ANXIOUSLY FREED

This book is dedicated to you.

ANXIOUSLY FREED

Advantage
BOOKS

TAMMY VERGE

Anxiously Freed by Tammy Verge
Copyright © 2020 by Tammy Verge
All Rights Reserved.
ISBN: 978-1-59755-601-9

Published by: ADVANTAGE BOOKS™
                  Longwood, Florida, USA
                  www.advbookstore.com

Author Photo by Spoiled Rotten Photography

Library of Congress Catalog Number: 2020942314

First Printing: August 2020
20 21 22 23 24 25   10 9 8 7 6 5 4 3 2
Printed in the United States of America

Table of Contents

Acknowledgments

First and foremost, I want to thank God for bringing me to where I am today! To my husband, Clint, you have been supportive and an inspiration to me from the day we met. Thank you for your love and encouragement as I wrote my story, and for assisting in the final revision and editing processes. To my family and friends that have stood with me throughout my entire journey, I send my love and appreciation for the lasting impact you have made in my life. Lastly, I am forever grateful for Onsite, my counselors, and the myriad of other resources that have provided me with guidance and direction during my journey of learning to *love myself.*

Preface

At forty-six years of age, I decided to write about my life, thus far, to help others that have struggled with similar issues in life. The topics will cover trauma, neglect, emotional abuse, mental abuse, physical abuse, codependency, betrayal, anger, grief, loneliness, lost spiritually, forgiveness, grace, breaking generational curses, molestation, alcoholism, domestic violence, fear, divorce, special needs, anxiety, depression, joy, courage, and healthy self-love.

My intent in writing this book is to tell my story. To share the joy, along with the pain. My audience is anyone that has, is, or will struggle with any of the above. To any friends or family reading this: Know that you were just part of the story. I love, appreciate, and accept each of you, for who and where you are in life! I wrote this story, as best as I possibly could, to illustrate my life from *my* perspective, including the thoughts and emotions I experienced *at the time* of the events. My desire is that by allowing myself to be open and honest about sharing my life, my story will help others. That my vulnerability will allow me to fully connect to my readers at an emotional level, as they relate to the experiences that I have shared.

Writing this book was very therapeutic for me. Recalling the ups and downs of my life experiences brought on a rollercoaster of emotions as I typed the words of this book. At times, there was pain and tears, but other times, there was joy and laughter. Through all of this, the thought of my story helping you gave me the courage to continue writing. As you read this book, know that *you* were on my mind, and I am speaking directly to you. I am with you as I share my life journey with you.

Some may ask if I would go back and change anything. I don't know the answer to that question. On the one hand, part of me wouldn't want to go through the hurtful experiences, but on the other hand, I know that those experiences have led me to exactly where I am today.

Chapter 1

A Whopping 3.5 Pounder!

I came into the world at 3½ pounds at Huntsville Hospital in Huntsville, Alabama! I was premature, and my lungs had not yet fully developed. It took me two months to gain just two pounds! I was born on October 27th, when my mother's due date wasn't until January 5th of the following year. Later in life, a family member jokingly told me that I was so tiny at birth that I had, in fact, "slid out!"

It wasn't until much later in life that I explicitly questioned why I was born prematurely. I only knew there were complications at my birth. I had assumed that it was because my mother, Deborah, was sixteen when I was born. That wasn't the reason. My father, Jack, was seventeen. He and my mother dated for a short time before they got married, and of course, they married because of me. I later learned that my maternal grandmother referred to my mom's pregnancy as "in trouble" and wouldn't use the word "pregnant." Grandmama, as I called her, was very old-fashioned.

I had to stay inside an incubator within Huntsville Hospital's Neonatal Intensive Care Unit (NICU) for over two months. Naturally, my entire immediate family was concerned about whether or not I would survive. It was an extremely stressful time and was a severe emotional toll on everyone. My family visited me as often as possible. My incubator happened to be one of the first ones to be donated to the hospital. My paternal grandmother, Mawmaw, told me that she remembered reading an article in the local newspaper about the donation. One time, while Mawmaw was visiting me, I stopped breathing. A nurse came over, pressed around my heart with two of her fingers, and my heart began beating again!

My mom's sister, Denise, would babysit me sometimes while my mom worked. Denise would have been about fourteen at the time. I have heard countless stories from my family members concerning my parent's courtship and the events that happened following my birth. My mom said that during her senior year in high school, she took me to school once, during her homeroom, to "show me off." She said she was so proud of me! My dad's sister, Wanda, shared homeroom with her that year and was at school the day my mom brought me.

Throughout my parent's tumultuous relationship, including before I was born, my dad was physically abusive to my mother. My mom's family didn't like my dad from the beginning. I can't say I blame them, based upon what I have heard about his behavior during this time of his life! My maternal grandparents that I refer to as "Grandmama" and "Granddaddy" were even involved in a physical altercation with my dad in my grandparent's front yard over my dad's behavior! After they were married, my parents eventually settled into an apartment near my mom's parents. My parent's marriage only lasted until I was about three-years-old. I do not have any recollection of this time, as I was too young and had yet to have my first memory.

My dad's sister, Sally, is only five years older than me. During my early years, my mom would occasionally babysit Sally so she could come to visit me. When I was much older, Sally shared with me that she remembered having a dream about her pushing my baby crib down the street to escape my house! Even she, as a little girl, had witnessed and had been impacted by my dad's violent behavior. During their short marriage, no one saw or experienced firsthand my dad's violent behavior more than my mother! My mom said that my dad only laid his hands on me one time. My mom was cooking, and I was crying in my highchair because I was hungry. My dad reached over and slapped me on my leg. My mom said that she wanted to take the pan of hot grease from the stove, sling it on him, and hit him with the pan! However, she also knew that if he ever got up, there would be trouble! Mom said that this event was the last straw for her, and she left my dad. My understanding is that from this point on, I rarely had any contact with my dad. Mawmaw would continue having a good and steady relationship in my life. She tried her best to fill the void in my life that was left by my dad. I would only see my dad when I was visiting Mawmaw's house, but it was sporadic. Mawmaw said that my dad would often ask to see me, but when he had the opportunity, he would usually only spend fifteen to thirty minutes with me.

Granddaddy and Grandmama said that one thing they did admire about my dad was the fact that he had a good job when I was born, and that he paid off my entire hospital bill from my birth. It was in the double-digit thousands, which I am sure was considered a large amount of money back in 1973! However, this is also the same man who usually failed to pay the court-ordered $15/week in child support.

My mom came from a low-income, working-class family. After I was an adult, my mom told me that Granddaddy had signed over his entire paycheck from his job to settle her divorce from my father. I can't imagine how difficult that was for him to do, but I am willing to bet it was worth every penny to him. He was protecting his daughter and grand-daughter, and it gave him peace of mind that we would be able to move forward with our lives. I am sure that the combination of knowing what Granddaddy did, coupled with going through a divorce and becoming a single-parent at twenty-years-old, must have been devastating for my mother. She wanted to be finished with my dad and did what she believed was best for us.

Grandmama was a sales clerk at Woolworth's department store in Huntsville, and Granddaddy was in maintenance at the local Winn-Dixie supermarket. My mother and I moved in with them following the divorce, and we lived with them on and off throughout my childhood. They were more like "second parents" to me than grandparents. I always had a close relationship with Granddaddy. Mom told me a story about what Granddaddy told her as she was getting ready to bring me home from the hospital, which was right before Christmas. He said, "You better not let anyone hold that baby until I hold her!" I know this was the beginning of the special bond that Granddaddy and I would have for almost the next 35 years! He was a father-figure to me, especially since my dad was, for the most part, out of the picture growing up.

I've always heard that because I was the oldest grandchild (on both sides), a girl, and had complications when I was born, I was spoiled. I believe saying that I was "spoiled" during this time of my life would be an understatement! It may not have been with money, but it sure was with love, which is what truly counts. I never wanted for anything!

One of my first memories is of playing hide-and-seek with my Aunt Denise and Aunt Dianne at Grandmama and Granddaddy's house. I couldn't have been more than three-years-old, and they were both babysitting me. All I remember is looking around the entire house for both of them, and deciding to look *inside* the washing machine! This is funny to me because it was impossible for them to fit inside a washing machine. This shows just how large the world seems to a small child! I must have had the thought that if I could hide in the washing machine, then they could hide in it, as well.

My Aunt Denise had a blonde-headed doll on roller skates that she kept in a box, located inside of Grandmama's linen closet from when she was a young girl. She would have been a teenager at this time. Though the doll belonged to Denise, Grandmama allowed me to take the doll out of the box and play with it while Denise was not at home. I remember having an absolute blast playing with the doll and rolling it down the hallway, at least until Denise came home. She got upset when she caught me playing with it.

Granddaddy and Grandmama had a Great Dane named "Turk" at their house when I was a toddler. My mom said my uncle would sit me on Turk, and it looked like I was sitting on a horse! It would be almost an entire year before my first cousin, Gary, was born to my mom's sister, Dianne, and my Uncle Jesse. Here's a funny story about Gary and me when we were toddlers. We decided that it would be a good idea to try some of Turk's dry dog food to see how it would taste! I don't recommend it! I remember that Turk's giant bag of dog food always sat beside the back door. We each got a piece of dog food, popped it in our mouth, and quickly realized that we would *never* do that again. What in the world were we thinking? I suppose we were just curious and discovering things like all kids do growing up!

Dianne would also babysit me when I was little. Gary and I would play when I visited their house. We would play outside on his swing set and turn flips on the A-frame bar of the swing set. I remember how much Gary loved wearing his cowboy hat. Whenever it was lunchtime, we would sit on opposite ends of the kitchen table and make silly faces at each other. I don't remember this, but it is one of my uncle's favorite stories to tell about me: I was about two and a half years old, and Gary was about 18 months old. Jesse was home on leave from the Navy. Dianne was at work, and Jesse was at home watching us. Jesse was vacuuming the hallway, and he had the vacuum plugged into a wall outlet located inside the bedroom where Gary and I were playing. The vacuum all of a sudden shutoff, and Jesse walked into the bedroom to see what had happened. Jesse saw me standing next to the outlet with the end of the electric cord in my left hand. Jesse asked, "Who unplugged my vacuum?" I pointed at Gary, who was sitting on the floor at least six feet away playing with a truck, and I said, "Gary Lee did it!" Jesse still laughs, so hard, every time he tells this story!

I have a small memory box with items from my childhood. One of my prized childhood possessions is my baby book. Some of the contents include a lock of hair from my first haircut, my teeny-tiny hospital bracelet from my birth, and numerous birthday cards. The box also contains a yellow baby pillow that I used in my crib. It's disgusting to think about, but there is no telling what unimaginable things I did to it! Even after numerous washes, it still has some stains on it. Knowing how much I loved my baby pillow,

Mawmaw made me a custom pillowcase for it several years ago. Mawmaw loves to sew and crochet. She is so creative and enjoys making handmade gifts for family and friends.

I also have several photo albums containing countless photos taken of me as a baby and a young toddler. Although I don't recall many memories of my life before I was four-years-old, I have heard the stories associated with most of these pictures. One of my favorite baby pictures is of my mom and Dianne bathing me in the sink. In my earliest years, I was so loved and cared for in every direction.

Mawmaw still jokes that she and I had "burned up the roads" traveling back and forth from Huntsville to Iuka, Mississippi, to see her mother, my great-grandmother, Eula. We would also go to see my great-grandparents on my dad's side in Red Bay, Alabama, and my dad's sister, Donna, and her husband, Roger, who also lived in Iuka, Mississippi. Mom allowed Mawmaw to take me for visits, even when I was just a small baby. Mawmaw said that when we were staying with relatives, she would pull out a dresser drawer, set it on the floor, and make a bed out of it for me. She would also make a bed for me out of a banana box when we were traveling in the car. She said that I was such a "teeny little thing," and my great-grandparents would say, "You are gonna kill that baby!" I agree this was not safe, and doing this would especially be unheard of these days, with all of the current seat belt laws and car seats available. However, I do laugh to myself about this now, when I consider this was back in the days when you could ride in the bed of an open pick-up truck going down the highway, not wear a seat belt, and no one thought or cared a thing about it!

Even though Mawmaw worked long hours at the Lee jeans factory for years, she always found time to spend with me. She took care of me quite often, early on in my childhood. She has always said that I was like one of her own. Mawmaw had five children. Though I am forty-six, Mawmaw is still alive today, and she just turned eighty-four! I have lost count of how many grandchildren, great-grandchildren, and great-great-grandchildren she has now. I know it is in the double-digits for each!

I do not have any memories of Mawmaw's first husband, Jack Sr., during this time of my life. I called him, Papa Jack. I know he only saw me a few times in my life because Mawmaw and Papa Jack divorced soon after I was born. He was an architect and designed many schools in Huntsville and the surrounding areas. Papa Jack was very talented, but he was also an alcoholic. He died when I was ten years old of cirrhosis of the liver at the age of forty-nine. From what I understand, he didn't always treat my grandmother or some of his kids well, including alcohol-induced rages and physical abuse. Mawmaw told me, not long ago, that Papa Jack would sometimes throw massive tantrums at the ball field when my dad played baseball as a young boy. Mawmaw said that Papa Jack's public displays of anger would emotionally hurt and embarrass my dad and his younger brother, Perry.

Mawmaw would later marry my Papa Karl. He is a part of my earliest memories around four-years-old. Also, around this time, Alan would enter my life, which was my mom's second husband. Alan treated me like I was his own and referred to me as his "pride and joy." Soon after they married, we moved to Lynette, Alabama, for Alan's job. My first memory after moving to Lynette is when I almost swallowed a penny that I found soon after I had taken a bath. I remember the time when I thought it would be interesting to see what would happen if I mixed my talc powder in a pink swan with water from the kitchen sink! In case you're wondering, it just makes "rocks." Mom and Alan woke up soon after I completed my "experiment." I also enjoyed playing the piano at Mrs. Goggin's house, a nearby neighbor, as well as taking trips to the store across the street with some of the older girls in the area. I don't recall this, but Mom told me that she and I would cool our Brussels sprouts over the floor vents as we ate and watched television. These are all of the memories and stories that I remember from living in Lynette. After a few months, we moved back to Huntsville, and both Alan and Mom began working for a cafeteria called Piccadilly. My mom worked at Piccadilly for many years.

The first years of my life were unsettling and filled with change. Fortunately, I was too young to remember the turbulent times during this part of my childhood. However, many of the memories I do have were of happy times with family. I would soon learn of another significant change on the horizon that would forever change my life and would be met with a joyous expectancy.

Chapter 2

Oh, Brother!

I was four-years-old when we moved back to Huntsville from Lynette. We moved into a two-bedroom apartment that was near Grandmama and Granddaddy's house. Mom soon learned that she was pregnant with my little brother, Shaun! My first memory of this apartment was waking up one morning in my bed, afraid to move because I thought that there was a lion in my bed. Now, it doesn't make much sense, but to my barely five-year-old mind, believing I had a lion in my bed was serious business! I eventually got up the nerve to finally get out of bed after lying there motionless for a long while. Whew, no lion, after all!

Although this is my first memory of being afraid in bed, my fear of the dark started when I was a toddler. I required solid-colored sheets for me to sleep, even if I was sleeping with my mom. If the sheets had patterns or figures on them, I would go nuts! After the lights were out, I could still visualize those images in my head, and it would scare me! I cannot precisely pinpoint when most of my worrying in life turned to anxiety, but I do know my deepest fears go back as far as my earliest memories.

It was around this time that I began to have this regularly recurring dream. Even though I started having these dreams over forty years ago, and I can *still* recall them vividly. In my dream, it was nighttime, and I was a passenger in a black car. The car was driving on a road that was only lit up by the headlights. When I would look over to the driver's seat, there would be no driver! However, the steering wheel would be moving as if someone were actually driving. It scared the life out of me in my dream. When I started to realize that this dream was recurring, I remember becoming afraid to go to sleep at bedtime out of fear that this same dream would keep coming back. In my dream, I was entirely at the mercy of the non-existent driver, I didn't know where this car was taking me, I couldn't get out of the car, and I couldn't stop it! I don't precisely recall when these dreams ended, but they eventually did stop. I don't remember ever telling my mom about these dreams at the time they occurred, or why I didn't tell her most things when I was a young child.

I started going to preschool at a Baptist church that was near our apartment. It was at this preschool that I first started learning about God. I still remember one of my teachers, Mrs. Harris. My cousin Jeremy, Aunt Denise's son, and Shaun would have Mrs. Harris, as well! My favorite thing about preschool was recess, where I loved playing on the monkey bars and the see-saw! There was a tiny house on the playground that I also liked to play on. You could climb up one side of the house to the roof and then go down a slide on the other side of the house. I loved babies and was intrigued by them from an early age. I can remember going outside during recess and wanting to be near these two baby girls, in particular, that the teachers were caring for while we played on the playground. They were so cute! I also loved the snacks at preschool, and this is the first time I remember ever making Rice Krispy Treats, having an orange drink, and eating those little flower-shaped cookies with the hole in the middle that you can put your finger through to hold it. I loved it when Granddaddy would pick me up from preschool in his Winn-Dixie utility work truck. He would let me ride in the bed of the truck on the way to his house, which was less than a mile away.

The only time I remember ever getting in trouble at preschool was when I got curious about a toy. I'm sure you have seen the baby doll bottles with the fake milk inside of them. Well, this toy was similar but was a pitcher of syrup that went with a dish playset. I broke off the top of the pitcher, so I could see if it had real syrup inside. In case you're wondering, it wasn't real syrup!

One day after preschool, I brought home a name tag sticker with my name on it that said, "I cleaned my plate!" It had a bunch of gold stars on it and was displayed on Grandmama and Granddaddy's bulletin board in their house for *years*. I was so proud of it and thrived on the recognition I received from my grandparents.

On one particular road trip with Grandmama and Granddaddy, I *really* had to use the bathroom. There wasn't a place to stop, so Granddaddy had me go in a KFC bucket on the side of the road! On another trip, I was in a restaurant eating with Grandmama and Granddaddy. While I was eating, I happened to get ketchup all over the side of my arm. Granddaddy noticed it and told me to clean the ketchup off my arm. Of course, I cleaned it off with my tongue! Granddaddy laughed, so hard, at me when I did it.

When Mom was pregnant with Shaun, I would get so excited thinking about him being born. I would try to imagine what it was going to be like to be a "big sister" to him. One day, while we were walking up the stairs inside our apartment, I remember telling Mom that I came up with a great idea about Shaun. I told her that when he was born that I wanted to give him all of my Golden Books. The sacrifices we will make for those we love!

I always loved it when my mom would color in coloring books with me. I was so envious that she was so much better at it than me. She would take the crayons and outline the images in the book and then fill them in. I tried to color like Mom, but somehow my coloring seemed to look a lot like scribble-scrabble! Sometimes, I would take a red marker and only color in Barbie's lips, while leaving the rest of the page blank. I would do this throughout the entire coloring book!

Another thing that my mom would sometimes do that I thought was so cool was when she would collect the shavings out of my crayon box, place them between sheets of wax paper, and use an iron to make the colors melt and spread out in a kaleidoscope of colors. One time, I was in Mom and Alan's bedroom coloring and saw a "dirty magazine." I asked Mom about it, but I don't recall what she said, or if she could even really explain it. I just remember knowing it was "bad." This is my first memory of being exposed to anything of a sexual nature.

One of my favorite things to do with my mom, and sometimes Alan, when I was a young girl was going to Brahan Spring Park in Huntsville! This city park was unique in that it had child amusement park rides located inside the park. There was a small train that circled a pond that I loved to ride. If it doesn't seem like there are too many stories of my mom spending time with me, it is because she was working. Many times, she was working more than one job to make ends meet. I thrived on the attention she gave me, and this quality time is what I desired and needed to feel loved.

On October 23, 1978, my brother, Christopher Shaun, was born. My mother had complications at his birth, as well. The doctors rushed Shaun to a hospital in Atlanta, Georgia, when he was only twelve hours old because he had hemorrhaged and was convulsing. It is unclear exactly how it happened, but Shaun later developed Cerebral Palsy. Before Shaun was born, everything was about me. Afterward, and for obvious reasons, it became mostly about him.

As Shaun got older, Mom would take him to the local Cerebral Palsy Center in Huntsville for occupational, physical, and speech therapy. I would occasionally attend these sessions with them. As he got a little older, Shaun participated in some of the local Cerebral Palsy Telethons to raise money for children with Cerebral Palsy and research. Shaun had the opportunity to play on a baseball team where all of the players, like Shaun, had Cerebral Palsy. Our cousin, Jeremy, played for the opposing team. Unlike a regular game of baseball, Jeremy's team would assist Shaun's team during the game by pushing the wheelchairs around the bases, etc. Shaun was fortunate in that he never had to use a wheelchair or use leg braces like most of the other kids.

Shaun was the cutest! I was so proud of him! Mom told me one time that if he had been a girl, his name would have been Shannon. I told her that I wanted his name to be Frosty, as in the snowman! Shaun's birthday is just four days before mine. Since our birthdays are so close together, we would usually celebrate our birthdays together in a combined party throughout most of our childhood. We even had a few birthday cakes in my early years that were Halloween-themed cakes with pumpkins on them. All of the décor, including the tablecloth, paper plates, and napkins would match, as well.

I remember a time that we went to the local fair as a family. I won a goldfish playing the game where you toss a ring, and if it lands on or in your fishbowl, you win! Of course, I decided to name him "Goldie." How original, right? I remember going to bed that night, then waking up the next morning excited to see Goldie. When I came downstairs and went into the kitchen, I could see by the look on my mom's face that something was wrong. She was afraid to tell me that Goldie had died! I'm not sure why this didn't bother me, but I just shook it off and went on about my business, as if nothing was wrong.

Not too long after this, all four of us moved temporarily to Baton Rouge, Louisiana, for Alan's job. We only lived in Baton Rouge for a total of four months before moving back to Huntsville. I was in the first grade during this time. I *loved* Wonder Woman, and I remember Mom buying me a Wonder Woman light-blue plastic lunch box for school. It came complete with a Wonder Woman Thermos inside the lunch box. I loved it, and I took my lunch almost every day in my lunch box. I would usually have a sandwich and chips, with Kool-Aid in the Thermos. I also thought I was "cool" because I had Wonder Woman Underoos and Wonder Woman slipper socks! One of my favorite things to do while we lived in Baton Rouge was to ride my Big Wheel around our apartment complex. A neighbor gave me a cute pink coat to wear. One day, while I was outside riding around on my Big Wheel, a girl stopped me and said, "Hey, that's my coat!" She recognized her old coat that her mom had given me. I didn't understand why she was mad. I don't remember everything I said, but I knew it was *my* pretty pink coat now and she wasn't getting it back!

My first-grade teacher in Baton Rouge was Mrs. Houston. Well, Mrs. Houston left the classroom for a few minutes one day and left a student in charge to take the names of anyone talking. Well, I was one of those that got caught! I was so upset! I went up to the boy that was taking names, tried to convince him that it was unfair and that I should have another chance! He didn't care. I can't recall what happened when Mrs. Houston came back to the room, but I didn't get into trouble. I also experienced my first encounter with a bully in Mrs. Houston's class! I don't remember his name, but he sat on the row of chairs to my right. I had a brown book bag with a clown on it. One day, out of pure meanness, he took my bookbag and drew on it. I was so upset that I cried in the classroom. I despised this kid! I don't recall if he ever got in trouble for drawing on my bookbag.

In school, we had a fundraiser where we sold these skinny, milk chocolate candy bars with a Pizza Hut coupon on the back. We didn't venture too far, but Mom took me around to most of our neighbors in the apartment complex, trying to help me sell the candy bars. I remember being at school after the fundraiser was over and winning a Chinese yo-yo, while a girl named Carmen got a poster of a "hot" young celebrity boy. What a raw deal! Mom and I worked hard trying to sell those candy bars, but apparently, we didn't sell enough! Oh, the struggles of a first-grader!

I didn't see Alan much because of his work schedule, but I do remember attending a Christmas party at the home of his boss, Sandy. I remember Sandy's name because he was male, and it seemed strange to me that a man would have that name. Sandy, and his wife, were kind to me and gifted me with a baby doll for Christmas, which made me feel special!

We had a neighbor in our apartment complex named Richard. I remember Richard because he taught me a magic trick where you hold a towel in front of you and make your leg disappear. To perform the magic trick, you lift one of your legs while simultaneously raising the towel. It reminded me of what a rodeo clown does to a bull. It wasn't exactly magic, but to a first-grader, it sure was cool!

I wasn't used to living in a different place. I recall my first couple of days on the school bus being very traumatic! I didn't understand that our apartment complex had one centrally-located bus stop. On my first day riding the bus home, the driver drove *past* my apartment building and stopped at the bus stop. I was scared out of my mind! I thought I would never see my family again! I thought I would never get back home, and I would be lost forever! I threw a crying fit on the bus. I remember all of the other kids looking at me in amazement like, "Why is she so upset?" I soon came to expect that the bus driver would safely get me home, and I learned which pathway would lead me to where my mother was waiting on me outside of our apartment.

One day after school, I had a special surprise waiting for me when I started down the pathway towards my mom. This time, it wasn't only Mom waiting for me, but Granddaddy and Grandmama were also standing there with her! Oh, my goodness, I was so happy when I saw them! I will never forget it. I had not seen them in quite a while, so I took off running and jumped in Granddaddy's arms. Not long after their visit, we moved back to Huntsville, and into the same apartment complex that we had lived in before moving to Baton Rouge.

The next Christmas, one of my favorite gifts was a set of Barbie doll blow-up furniture. I loved playing with my Barbie dolls and furniture. It was also the same year that I got my first regular-sized bicycle! It was a yellow Huffy with a "banana" seat. It replaced a used, small pink bike with training wheels that Granddaddy bought for me at the local auction. Granddaddy and Uncle Jesse taught me how to ride on this little pink bike. Alan took me outside to the apartment complex parking lot and showed me how to ride my new bicycle. Of course, I fell a few times, but I got right back up and kept going. Before long, I was allowed to go outside, by myself, and ride my bike.

During this time of my life, I enjoyed playing with my many different toys. I had an Easy-Bake oven that required a particular light bulb to use the oven part. I am not sure why we never got one, but it didn't matter to me. I mixed the cake mixes with water and ate the mix straight out of the packets. It still tasted good to me! I also loved playing with a Slinky, Silly Putty, a Jacks & Ball set, my skateboard, a Milky the Marvelous Milking Cow toy, and my Play-Doh hair salon set. The Play-Doh hair salon set was so much fun! I had a Barbie Doll perfume maker set, to go with all of my other Barbie toys! Grandmama kept several of the older vintage Barbie dolls from when my mom and her sisters were little girls. I loved to play with these dolls, too. I remember making a bed for my Barbie dolls out of stacks of small romance novels lying around the house. We had a The Green Machine Big Wheel that I rode at my grandparent's house. I also had a metal kitchenette set in my room that was so loud when I played with it. Everyone thought it was so funny when Shaun would hide in the bottom of the cabinets and the refrigerator.

I remember being excited about my mom taking me to the local K-mart. I think I bought a Ken doll before I even had my first Barbie doll! Mom would explain to me sometimes before we went to the store, "Now, just because we are going to the store, doesn't mean we always have to buy something." I was probably thinking, "Yeah, whatever you say, Mom!" I enjoyed buying toy high heels, but one of my favorite things to buy was blue Barbie doll eyeshadow! Of course, this was back when blue eyeshadow was the "in" thing!

About this time, I learned how to play the card game UNO, and would play with my family and friends. Mom and Alan would sometimes invite people over to play. One of my favorite things that I had in my room was a record player that played 45's. I had the record *"It's a Small World,"* but my favorite was by Bert and Ernie from *Sesame Street* with Ernie singing "Rubber Ducky." I would listen to these records while I played in my room. Oh, the things you can remember from your childhood, but then you can't seem to remember anything as a middle-aged adult!

Not long after we moved back to Huntsville, I met Brian. Brian was Alan's son from a previous marriage. Brian came to stay with us one night, and he ran away. We eventually found him walking back home to his mom's house. I imagine that he was scared since he had never stayed the night with us before. We would occasionally see Brian when we would visit Alan's mother, Nanny. Although we did not see Brian much growing up, we were able to reconnect several years later. Nanny didn't live far from our apartment. Sometimes, Mom and I would walk to Nanny's house to see her. One time, while we were walking to Nanny's, I wanted to stop because I was tired. We happened to stop in front of the house of a nice elderly lady. She saw us and invited us inside for a drink and a snack. She had a box of Crispy Kreme donuts on the table. Who can resist a Crispy Kreme donut? I *had* to have one of those!

Nanny always had a few of my favorite things at her house, too! She had a white candy dish in the living room that *always* contained plain M&M's, and Bubble Yum bubble gum in her "candy drawer." She had a yellow booster seat that I liked to use when I got to sit at the "adult" table. I had my fourth birthday party at Nanny and her husband, Granddaddy George's house. I remember crying when everyone sang "Happy Birthday" to me. I don't know why I cried. Nanny always treated me like I was one of her own, though Shaun was her blood-related grandchild, and I wasn't.

Shaun and I had a babysitter named Pam that lived nearby on Redstone Arsenal. Pam seemed strange to me as a little girl! I didn't understand why she shook a lot and didn't drive. I always felt super uncomfortable around her. She made us eat either mushroom soup or peanut butter sandwiches for lunch, and I can't stand mushrooms to this day! I even got tired of eating peanut butter sandwiches! Shaun was still little, and I remember that I would often lie down with him to get him to sleep for naps. He was the sweetest boy when he was little!

As a young girl, I remember struggling to understand certain things about my father and why I felt like something was missing. I say struggling because I knew I had a biological father that wasn't in my life, but I did have a father-figure in Alan and with my Granddaddy. I didn't understand why exactly my biological father wasn't in my life. I used to daydream about being in a room where Alan would be sitting in one chair, my real dad, Jack, in another chair and having to choose which one was going to be my dad.

It caused me great confusion, as I was too young to understand the dynamics between my family and my birth father. When I would ask questions about my dad, my mom would tell me that I would understand when I got older. Mom told me growing up that I would get so mad when she said terrible things about him. I imagine so, as he was technically the other half of me. This "bad" man that everyone referred to made up the other half of me, and there wasn't anything I could do about it. I was associated with him, whether I wanted to be or not. No part of me thinks my mom would ever want me to feel this way, but I felt ashamed of him. I also felt shame within myself because I was associated with him.

I still have many memories of when the four of us, Mom, Alan, Shaun, and me, were together as a family. One of my favorite things to eat was Alan's barbeque sandwiches that he would make in the oven. Now and then, he would let me take a few sips of his coffee, or more accurately, he allowed me to take a few sips of his coffee-flavored creamer and sugar. Alan drank a large amount of beer. I know this because I would save the empty beer cans for money. Granddaddy would take me to turn the beer cans in for cash. I would use this cash for "fun" money. Sometimes, Granddaddy would take me, Shaun, and a few of my other cousins. Gary, Chris, and Jeremy would sometimes go with us to turn in the cans. Gary and Chris are my Aunt Dianne and Uncle Jesse's sons. Dianne and Jesse also have a daughter, Rebecca. Shaun, Jeremy, and Rebecca are all about the same age.

One of my favorite stories to tell about my childhood has to do with Granddaddy: When I was five, Granddaddy experienced some back issues and was in Huntsville Hospital recovering from his surgery. Mom took Shaun and me up to the hospital to see him, but I had to leave because they were about to remove his staples. Since I knew I was about to leave the hospital and kids weren't allowed to stay for his procedure, I looked over at the box-shaped landline telephone in his room and memorized the phone number on it. Even at five, I knew what I was about to do! After the hospital visit was over, Shaun and I went to Nanny's house for her to babysit us. When we arrived at Nanny's house, I got on the phone and dialed the number while she was changing Shaun's diaper. Nanny didn't see what I was doing at the time. A nurse picked up the phone and asked me where my mom was and to put her on the phone. I responded to her, "She's there with you!" The next thing I knew, my mom was on the phone getting onto me and asking about Nanny. Nanny came into the room, asked me what I was doing, and got on the phone with my mom. I can't exactly remember what happened after that, but all I knew was that I was going to check on my Granddaddy!

Granddaddy was a member of a club called the Fraternal Order of Eagles in Huntsville. The only thing I know about this organization is that Granddaddy took us there at Easter and Christmas. At Christmas, we each had our names called, saw Santa, and received a gift! One of the most memorable times I had with Granddaddy was when he took me there for an Easter Egg Hunt. I found so many eggs on the hunt and significantly more than some of the other kids. When I proudly showed Granddaddy all of my eggs, he told me that since I found so many eggs, I should share some of them with the other children that may not have found as many as me. Now, as spoiled as I was at times, I never forgot that he said this to me. I can recall him saying this to me as if it were yesterday. He was planting seeds, for sure!

One of the things I enjoyed doing with my mom around Easter was coloring eggs. One year, she bought me a beautiful Easter dress that had bells sewn into the underside of the skirt so they weren't visible while I was wearing it. A picture of me in this dress is my favorite Easter picture that I have of myself growing up.

When I was growing up, cereal companies put toys in the cereal boxes. As strange as it sounds, I remember getting miniature plant kits from inside a box of cereal! I think you were only required to add water to it! Grandmama saved the proof of purchase coupons on the cereal boxes and sent them in for us to get prizes in the mail.

One of my favorite bath toys growing up was a blonde-headed baby doll that Mom bought me. If you got soap in the doll's hair and squeezed her tummy, the doll's hair would make these gigantic bubbles on her head! I loved taking baths with this doll.

I remember beginning to develop a little bit of an attitude around the age of five. One time, I got in trouble and was being punished by having to stay in my room. I think I had gone "out of bounds," referring to the distance I was allowed to go while playing outside at the apartment complex. I was sent straight to my room and wasn't able to get my skateboard and bring it inside. When I looked out my window, I saw a little girl playing with *my* skateboard! I threatened her and told her that she had better get off of my skateboard and that I would be down shortly to get it back! Another time, my mom's brother, Eddie, had called while my mom was in the shower. Shaun and I were in the living room, and I was *really* into watching my cartoons. When Eddie called the first time, I was already upset that he interrupted my cartoon watching! Well, he called again, and I just hung up on him! How dare he call while I was watching *my* cartoons!

Around this time is when I started to see that Shaun had struggles because I remember trying to "fix" the situation. I noticed that when Shaun would watch TV, his head would sway back and forth. I knew, even as a young child, that something had happened when he was born and that some things were different about him, but I never understood why. Once, while Shaun was watching television, I tried to keep his head from swaying. I thought if I helped him and taught him to hold his head straight, it would stop. I put my hands on his head to support it and held it steady for a few seconds. Once I let go, it wasn't long before his head started swaying again. It was at this point that I knew Shaun truly couldn't help it and that I couldn't fix the situation. I was five-years-old and just didn't know how to comprehend it all. For years, I was secretly mad at God for not giving me a brother that I *thought* should be like a "normal" or "regular" brother. I *still* struggle, at times, not understanding *why* God allowed Shaun to develop Cerebal Palsy and *how* everything fits into His plan. It's not that I love Shaun any less, but I don't want him to suffer in *any* way.

I began noticing Mom and Alan fighting more and more. One fight was so bad that Mom took Shaun and me and began leaving the apartment. Alan was arguing with her that he wanted me to stay with him. Mom eventually left with both of us, and I remember her driving us to her friend, Beth's house. Beth and her husband, R.L., had two sons, Mat, and Nick. The boys were the same ages as Shaun and I. I was in tears over the fighting when we arrived at Beth's house. These types of arguments continued between Mom and Alan and only increased over time.

The four of us eventually moved into a three-bedroom apartment within the same apartment complex. However, not long after we moved into the new apartment, Mom and Alan divorced. I was seven when they divorced, and to me, it seemed like Alan was there with us one day, and gone the next.

Chapter 3

Seven and Like No Heaven!

For me, the ages of seven to twelve would be some of the most hurtful and terrible times of my life. Not all of it, but enough of it was…

When Alan and Mom divorced, Alan moved into a two-bedroom apartment at a different complex across the street. The next thing I knew, Mom had a new boyfriend, and Alan had a new girlfriend, which was very painful for me. I was confused and didn't understand. I only knew about the fighting, name-calling, etc., leading up to their divorce, but when I started questioning why they got divorced, both Mom and Alan accused each other of infidelity. I remember thinking that not only did I not have my real dad in my life, but now I wouldn't have Alan in my life, at least not in the way it was before they divorced.

Sometimes, Shaun and I would stay with Alan and his girlfriend, J.L., on the weekend. We usually only stayed for one night, and when they had us, we never went anywhere. We never left the apartment! While we were there, they wouldn't spend quality time with us. They essentially acted as if we weren't even there with them, and would mostly drink and watch television. I can't remember exactly when it began, but when Alan would tuck Shaun and me in bed, he would "kiss us to death." When he did this, he would use his tongue like he was playfully attacking us with it. At first, it seemed funny and cute, until it wasn't. The frequency to which he would do this increased over time.

I remember starting to worry when I saw my mom drinking. I never knew of her to have a problem, but I knew what it was, and that alcohol could make people drunk. I asked her once about a particular drink she was drinking, and she informed me that it would take many of those to make her drunk. Her answer didn't make me feel any better or more at ease.

My mom's friend, Beth, would sometimes watch Shaun and me, which meant that we began to spend a lot more time with Mat and Nick! We always had so much fun together. Some of my favorite memories, from this period of my life, involved them. We went to each other's birthday parties, and one time, they had a bounce house to play in. The four of us would play *Star Wars* for hours and enjoyed playing "store." Mat would pretend like Shaun was an "old man" that came into the store to buy things. I would usually run the cash register. Mat would set out a jar next to the cash register to raise funds for Cerebral Palsy! Of course, Shaun would always donate the play money in the donation jar. It was so sweet!

Beth and Mat were both "book smart" and enjoyed playing the game Trivial Pursuit. Sometimes, Mom liked playing it, too. One time, I had asked Mom a question about something while she was playing Trivial Pursuit at our apartment. Beth and Mat were not there, but it wouldn't have mattered if they were. My mother's response to me was, "If Mat and Beth heard you ask that question, they would laugh at you!" She may not recall saying this, but her words hurt me to the core! I felt shame, I felt stupid, and I felt not good enough!

For whatever reason, Mom would make it a point to tell Shaun and me before entering a store together, "Now don't you get in here and *embarrass* me!" It was to the point that I remember asking my mother on several occasions, "Mom, was I good today?" or "Were we good today?" I remember continually wanting her attention and validation. I wanted to be "good enough" for her, but I didn't feel like I was for most of my life. Children naturally believe what their parents say about them. It is difficult to change how you view yourself if you were conditioned to believe certain things from such a young age.

I remember that Beth and Mom allowed Mat and I to go to a woman's home to attend something similar to Vacation Bible School. It sticks out to me significantly, because it was there that I learned my very first Bible verse, *"In My Father's house are many mansions; if it were not so, I would have told you. I go to prepare a place for you. And if I go and prepare a place for you, I will come again and receive you to Myself; that where I am, there you may be also."* (John 14:2-3 – NKJV)

Later, I was able to attend Vacation Bible School at a local church. One day, a yellow Sunday school bus stopped at my apartment complex. The side of it read "West Huntsville Baptist Church." The minister that was driving spoke to several parents around the complex, including my mom, to offer an invitation for their children to attend Vacation Bible School at the church. Mom told me I could go! I remember one of my teachers vaguely, as well as meeting in a room full of adults and kids where the ministers were talking and praying. It was a week filled with activities, and I had so much fun. There has never been a single time in my life that I have attended a church service with my mom. Despite this, throughout my childhood, seeds were being planted inside of me as I gained more exposure to church and had opportunities to learn about God. I am thankful and appreciative that I was able to attend church functions and learn about God, even though I have never been to a church service with my mom.

I always loved being able to stay at my Aunt Denise's house, with her and her son, Jeremy. I enjoyed reading to him and did this often when I stayed with Aunt Denise. Jeremy was so smart, even at a young age. He knew every word in his books! If I ever tried to take a short-cut and skip over anything, he would let me know it! Jeremy had a Cabbage Patch doll that his paternal grandmother had given him. I remember being envious and wishing that I had one. Later, I did receive a Cabbage Patch Kid for my birthday from my mom. Cabbage Patch dolls were the craze at the time, and nearly every kid wanted one of these dolls. Another great memory I have about my Aunt Denise is the time that she took me to see the play, *Annie*. We had such a great time, and I even wore my "Annie" dress!

Shaun and I had many different babysitters during this time, some more regular than others. Mom didn't have a choice, because she was a single-mom and both of my grandparents worked, as well. I guess it was whoever my mom could find at the time to watch us while she worked. There was one babysitter that lived in our apartment complex. I couldn't stand her! The first time we ever met her, she answered the door naked from the waist down and was still pulling up her pants to cover herself. Needless to say, it was more than any child should see! Thankfully, she only watched us a few times. Shaun was still little and was often asleep when we stayed with her, as well as other babysitters. One day, this same babysitter had some of her friends visiting, and they thought it would be a good idea to tie me up to see if I could get out of it. Her husband was in the Army, and he was at work when they did this to me. I didn't fight back. They sat there, watching me struggle and made fun of me. I have no idea why she thought it was a good idea to do this to me, or why her friends would get a kick out of it. I vaguely remember this happening to me, and I can't recall what I was feeling at the time they tied me up and teased me. I just remember that it wasn't a good feeling.

Another babysitter that I vividly remember lived around the corner from my grandparents. The mother in the family would watch Shaun and me. However, if she left to run errands on the arsenal nearby, her daughters would watch us. Most days, I would play outside with a water dish of soap and my baby dolls, play dress-up with some of the mother's pantyhose, or play with their dachshund named Chico.

One day, while the mother was gone, her youngest and middle daughter were at home watching Shaun and me. Shaun was sleeping, and the youngest daughter took me in a back room and locked the door. I do not ever recall her touching me, but she required me to touch her breasts. She made it into a type of game with me, trying to coerce or trick me into touching her. I know she locked the door because when she wouldn't unlock the door for her sister, the sister picked the lock with a bobby pin! This same youngest sister would also take me to the bathroom with her, sit me on top of her lap while she was sitting on the toilet, and play the same type of game with me. I remember feeling very afraid and extremely uncomfortable. She made me promise never to tell anyone. Later on, I remember her riding me around on her bicycle, and she asked me, "You never told anyone what we talked about, did you?" I told her that I hadn't.

The horrible things she did never came out until a few years later. I saw a story on the local news when I was in middle school about a teacher that had molested a child. I went into the den at my grandparent's house and cried. There was no way that my mom could have known what was going on, but my mom and Aunt Denise could see that something was severely upsetting me. I was terrified of telling them what had happened to me for two reasons: One, I knew that my Aunt Denise had gone to school and had been friends with some of these sisters, and second, I knew that my family would confront the youngest sister! I felt so ashamed, embarrassed, and humiliated. All I could think was, "Why me? Why did it have to be me?" Though later on, I knew deep down that I had done absolutely nothing wrong, I still had these questions! After telling Mom and Aunt Denise what had happened, I remember seeing Mom at the front door of Grandmama's house arguing and yelling with the youngest daughter, as I was walking up with my friend, Susan. Mom said the girl denied it, and that she couldn't understand why this was all coming out now. I had been afraid, so I had kept it buried deep down for as long as I could. Over the years, I had learned to hide some of my feelings. As I grew older, these buried feelings would come out, and I would rage!

Something else happened at this particular babysitter's house. One day, while the mother went to the store, there was a knock at the door. One of the daughters opened the door. It was a man with dark hair. He said, "Is your mom home?" The girls replied, "No." The girls didn't recognize him, so they shut the door and locked it. I remember being afraid and worrying about Shaun, who was asleep in the playpen in the back room. The daughters suspected that this strange man was the "Southwest Molester"! At the time, this man was all over the local news. During the late 1970s, eighteen women on the westside of Huntsville had been beaten, molested, and raped. No one was able to confirm that the man at the door was the "Southwest Molester," but everyone that heard the story suspected it was him. I recall standing in the living room while the door was open and staring at him in fear. I couldn't have been any older than seven. Around this same time, the mother took me over with her to a girlfriend's house in the area, and there was a large knife stuck in one of her trees. I overheard them talking and saying that they suspected that the "Southwest Molester" had left the knife in her tree. The police eventually caught a man they believed was the "Southwest Molester." He was convicted and is still in prison today.

I started to realize that I was an attractive little girl, even at seven or eight years old. My mom later told me that people said to her that she should have entered me in pageants, but she didn't because she thought that it would change me. I recall one incident where some Iranian men that lived a few doors down wanted to take my picture. They took my photo with a Polaroid camera that was popular at the time, and let me keep the photo.

I learned that Santa Claus was not real when I was seven. At Christmas, I received a carrying case for my Strawberry Shortcake dolls at my mom's. I knew something was wrong when I saw the *same* box at Alan's apartment. Eventually, Mom had to explain to me that there was, in fact, no Santa Claus. I imagine that all of the upheaval and distressful events were just happening too close together. It was overwhelming for a seven-year-old. While there were going to be many happy times, unfortunately, things would get worse.

If you remember, Shaun and I would have combined birthdays and share a birthday cake. As we got older, Mom would alternate buying our birthday cakes decorated with either Shaun's favorite, *The Dukes of Hazzard*, or Strawberry Shortcake, which I loved. I collected as many Strawberry Shortcake toys and other memorabilia, as I possibly could, as a little girl. When my birthday or Christmas came, I usually knew I would get something Strawberry Shortcake. I say this because not only did I love Strawberry Shortcake, but I would go up and smell the wrapped present. Since all of the various dolls smelled like different fruits, all I had to do was to see if the present smelled like fruit. If it did, then I knew it was something to do with Strawberry Shortcake. It was that easy!

One birthday, I got a Strawberry Shortcake cottage, sleeping blanket, watch, and an assortment of dolls! I couldn't have been happier! I liked Barbie dolls, too, but not as much as Strawberry Shortcake. Even though my dad wouldn't attend or have a birthday party for me, Mawmaw was invited and would find a way to be there.

On Saturday mornings, Mom would sit us in front of the television to watch cartoons and eat our favorite cereal. Mom referred to Shaun as a "cereal freak" because he loved eating it so much! Of course, Shaun had a *The Dukes of Hazzard* TV tray, and I had a Strawberry Shortcake TV tray that covered our laps while we ate our cereal.

Shaun loved small Matchbox cars! We would play with his cars on the floor. I would take my crayons and line them up to make roads or a parking lot for him. Sometimes, when I would aggravate Shaun, he would throw his cars at me to fight back! I have my quirks, but Shaun was particular about some things, too. He would get mad when the toe edge lining of his socks wouldn't line up on his feet correctly! So much so, he'd take his socks off! When Shaun tried to do this, he would start pulling at the toe end, which would make it hard for the whole sock to come off, and often left it caught up on his ankles!

One day, Mom, Shaun, and I went out to eat at Wendy's. Shaun couldn't have been much more than about two years old. We happened to be the only patrons in the restaurant. Mom was ordering our food, and she asked Shaun and me to find a table. Shaun, being a stubborn two-year-old, didn't like the one I chose, so he started arguing with me and loudly called me an "ugly" word! He was so loud that Mom heard him at the ordering counter on the other side of the restaurant! When she heard him, she hurried over, grabbed up Shaun, and they visited the restroom to "address" what he had called me. It wasn't funny at the time, but we enjoy telling and teasing each other about it now.

I recall meeting my mom's new boyfriend on the very night that she told me she had a boyfriend. Shaun was two, and I was seven. I didn't like him, nor did I really like Alan's new girlfriend. Sometimes, I would go to my mom's room, just to get her attention. I remember one time going in her room, when her boyfriend was over, to ask her a silly question about how a cape went on my Princess Leah doll. She knew what I was doing and brushed me off. Sometimes, her boyfriend watched us, and I didn't like this either.

I was desperate to get her attention and validation. So much, that I even made her a wooden paddle that said "Happy Mother's Day" on it! Who does that? Growing up, she was the only person that I can recall that spanked me as a child. Neither of the initial relationships that Mom and Alan had following their divorce lasted very long. Eventually, those two people would be out of our lives, as well. I started seeing Mom going down a path that I didn't like. This path was not one that was familiar to me, and that I wasn't going to take it lightly. Sometimes, other family members, including Granddaddy, would say comments about some of the choices my mother was making in front of me. It embarrassed me and made me feel even more resentful and angry with her. I don't recall my exact age when the following events occurred, but I do know that I was still in elementary school.

When I was a little girl, I would have cramps in my legs at night. They would hurt so bad that I would cry. Sometimes, Mom would rub my legs to help ease the pain. I would also get sick and have to vomit in the bathroom. Mom wouldn't always get up with me. She would just tell me to wet a washcloth with cold water and place it on my forehead.

I had long brown hair and was very tender-headed. Mom would get frustrated with me because I couldn't get all the shampoo out when I took a shower. Her doing this upset me so much that I began asking Mom to get a shorter haircut from a hairdresser that lived in a nearby apartment. When Granddaddy found out I wanted short hair, he jokingly told my mom that if she ever cut my hair, he would shoot her.

I shared a bed with Shaun until I was in middle school. Shaun would often urinate in the bed, and he always kept his Matchbox cars under his pillow. He would play with them at night, even after it was time to go to sleep. It wasn't unusual for me to wake up after I had rolled over on his cars in the middle of the night. Shaun would sometimes hit his head so hard on the headboard, and he wouldn't even cry! I never understood how hitting head so hard didn't seem to bother him, and I always just assumed that it was due to his Cerebral Palsy.

I remember that there were times that I would wake up, get myself ready for school, and walk to my elementary school, which was a couple of miles away. Most mornings, Mom would get up with us, but not every morning, especially if she had a boyfriend that stayed the night.

Around Christmastime one year, I didn't want to sing a Christmas song in music class. I detested having to sing it because it was a time in my life that I was unhappy. I had started attending this particular elementary school when I was in the second grade, and it was tough for me to fit in. I did my best to fit in, but I was an "outsider." When I would try to play with a few of the other girls during recess (they also had Strawberry Shortcake dolls), they weren't very accepting or welcoming.

One day, I went to the nurse's station at school, pretending to be sick. I don't remember why I did this or why I wanted to go home. The school called Mom at work. She came up to the school, but I couldn't go home. I had to stay at school, and she went back to work.

Throughout my elementary school years, Mom went through a series of different boyfriends. I don't remember much about them, but I do recall one specific time that I overheard Mom telling one of her friends that she suspected her boyfriend had stolen her rent money. I remember worrying about what was going to happen to us. I also remember worrying when I heard of incidents involving my mom's job. There were times that she would be interviewed at her work because someone had stolen money, and once, she had gotten in trouble by her manager for refusing to take off her jewelry for work. Although I knew that she would never steal or do anything to jeopardize her employment, I was worried that she might lose her job. I just wasn't able to understand these types of things. I was only in elementary school, yet I consistently had worrisome thoughts, such as these!

I enjoyed being able to go to the convenience store for my mom. When she needed something, she would sometimes allow me to walk to a convenience store that was just down the street from our apartment complex. A laundromat and hair salon sat between the apartment complex and the store. Grandmama would use this hair salon from time to time, and I would occasionally see her in there on my way to the store. If I didn't see Grandmama in the hair salon, there were times that I would stop at a payphone located on the street corner and call her. At this time, not only did kids not have to wear a seatbelt, but they were also allowed to buy cigarettes! I would usually buy her Tareyton 100 cigarettes, and a 16 oz. glass bottle Coca-Cola or a Tahitian Treat Fruit Punch drink. I would occasionally buy myself some "candy" cigarettes, and I loved getting *Archie* comic books to read! Sometimes, Mom would ask me to buy *The Huntsville Times* newspaper. She would get mad if I accidentally came back with the *Huntsville News* newspaper. I'm sure that the store clerk classified me as a "regular" since I went to the convenience store so often.

When I was at Grandmama and Granddaddy's, I would sometimes walk to the store near their house to buy groceries, usually a 2-liter Coca-Cola, or bread. Most of the time, I rode my bicycle and stopped at the Ben Franklin store, where I bought candy or a small toy. I would get something like one of those wooden paddles with the little ball that is attached by a rubber band or an over-sized balloon with the massive rubber band on the end of it!

Granddaddy's barbershop was nearby these stores. It was just around the corner in a shopping complex. I enjoyed going with my Granddaddy to get his hair cut and remember that the barbershop even had a shoe-shining booth. Alessandro's bakery, where my Aunt Denise used to work, was located in the same shopping complex. She gave me a Pillsbury Doughboy plastic doll from the bakery. I lost the original one, but I was able to find one just like it in an antique mall. I still have it in my memory box!

Since Mawmaw lived just a few miles from us, I was able to visit her and Sally often. Sometimes, I was able to spend the night. Mawmaw spoiled me rotten! I loved to play dress-up at her house. I did my best to walk around in her Candies high heels and wore her wigs around the house. She even gave me some of her used lipstick tubes and other cosmetics. Mawmaw was more of a free spirit, whereas my Grandmama was more old-fashioned and strict. However, I do remember that Grandmama did have a bright pink shade of lipstick that would be comparable to the MAC Brand of Candy Yum-Yum! Mawmaw would let you get away with far more than Grandmama! After I went back home to Mom from visiting Mawmaw, Mom would complain that my behavior had changed. She said that I would come back with an attitude and act differently. I'm not saying that she wasn't correct, but I certainly didn't like it when she got onto me for it. Mawmaw always seemed to have time for me and gave me tons of attention.

Papa Karl was gone quite a bit. I vaguely remember seeing or hearing things going on around this time that seemed strange to me, but I never gave it too much thought. Later, I learned that my Papa was a bookie, as in a sports-betting bookie. For a while, the money was rolling in, and they were living the good life.

Mawmaw and Papa Karl were even members of the local country club. When we would go to the country club, Papa Karl usually enjoyed playing poker in the bar area. Believe it or not, I even remember seeing my Papa Karl and my Papa Jack, Mawmaw's first husband, in the same lounge at the country club playing poker together! I remember being so confused about how I could have *two* Papas on the same side of the family! While Papa Karl played poker, Mawmaw and I would hang out at the swimming pool. This pool is where Mawmaw's friend, Sheila, taught me how to swim. Mawmaw would offer me $20 if I swam the entire length of the pool. That was a bunch of money to a little girl back then, and it bought me a ton of candy!

I always had and enjoyed Mawmaw's attention. Sometimes, she would come to pick me up, and the two of us would get a hamburger, go to the grocery store, and then get a double scoop of Baskin-Robbins ice-cream. She loved me, so much, as I did her.

It would take me years to figure out all of the family dynamics on my dad's side of the family! It was like trying to piece together a monstrous jig-saw puzzle. I heard about all these stories from Mawmaw. For instance, I learned that I had a half-sister, Amanda, from my dad. Then, he had four boys with another woman. Over the years, my dad would marry several times and have several kids. Shaun and I grew up together, and for the longest time, I had no idea exactly how all of these other people were related to me, much less how my dad was a father to some of them, but not to *me*! I would eventually meet the four boys, Jackie, Jonathan, Jamie, and Jasper. All four were from the same woman, Trish, which my dad would end up marrying multiple times. My dad, and his current wife, Sharon, have been married for over twenty years. I have one half-brother, Josh, from their relationship. One of the things that I admire most about Mawmaw is that she has always accepted and treated Shaun as one of her grandchildren, though he technically isn't blood-related.

Granddaddy enjoyed dabbling in gambling, too. Before going to school for appliance and refrigeration repair and working at Winn-Dixie, he served in the Army. He was a proud member of The Veterans of Foreign Wars (VFW). After he retired from Winn-Dixie, Granddaddy would go to the VFW so often that Grandmama and the rest of the family called it his "work." Most of the time, he would stay there all day, except for coming home for lunch! We later learned that Granddaddy was playing cards with other members while he was at the VFW! I've also heard stories that when Granddaddy was younger, he hustled pool to make ends meet a few times.

I did discover some things in elementary school that I did very well! I excelled in Spelling, Math, English, Art, and hurdle-jumping! I knew I'd get you with that last one! I had no idea that I was good at hurdle-jumping until we had a field day, and I scored very high for my age! I would enter spelling bees, though I wouldn't win, I was always one of the final contestants. Like most elementary-aged kids, I loved recess. Our school allowed us to do things that most kids can't do today. One of these things was flying kites. I loved my Donald Duck kite that Grandmama bought me! I flew it so high once that I was late coming back to class from recess because it took me forever to get my kite down. I began to realize that I was creative and loved art! I loved to draw and use colors. Grandmama was creative, too, and even made me several outfits on her sewing machine when I was a young girl. I'm positive that I got some of my creativeness from both of my grandmothers.

It was also at this time that Shaun, Jeremy, Rebecca, Chris, and Gary (all of my cousins on my mom's side), and I were in the same elementary school. Grandmama was so proud that all of her grandchildren were in the same school, that she bought the school annual one year because it had all of our pictures in it! Gary and I were in the fifth grade, Chris was in third, and Shaun, Jeremy, and Rebecca were in kindergarten.

Since Grandmama worked at Woolworth's Department store, she always made sure we had loose-leaf school notebook paper and other school supplies! Whenever I would go to Woolworth's, I liked to ride the mechanical toy horse and carousel that were near the entrance to the store. When I had some loose change to spare, I would occasionally go to the school supply store to buy Scratch N' Sniff stickers that smelled like fruit, or some uniquely shaped pencil erasers.

Grandmama loved all of her grandkids, but at times, she treated Shaun a bit differently. Everyone did because he was special and different. Sometimes, she would take up for Shaun when he was doing something he shouldn't be doing to other kids. He would get away with things, especially when it came to Grandmama. I know that Grandmama loved me, too. At times, she'd affectionately call me her "baby doll." She would jokingly say, "I'm going to turn you over on my checkered apron!" I knew she wasn't going to spank me! Both Grandmama and Granddaddy were always there for me, especially when my mom wasn't or couldn't be there. Since mom worked so much, Grandmama would consistently do things like bring me a set of clothes for a play that I was participating in at school.

I could always count on Grandmama. Others could, as well. She sacrificed so much throughout her life for those she loved. In short, Grandmama lived a hard life, especially with how she grew up. She had a lot of responsibility at a very young age, and in my mind, she deserved way more back out of life than she ever received. I had conversations with her, at times, when she would be very depressed. She would just sit and cry. When I was younger, I didn't fully understand or know about the things she experienced throughout her life or how it was affecting her. As I began to hear and learn more about Grandmama's backstory, the things I saw and heard during my childhood made much more sense.

When I was in my late twenties, Grandmama would make lunch several times a week, and I would often leave for lunch from my nearby job to join her and Granddaddy. These were special times that I will always cherish! Some of my most memorable moments during these difficult years of my life were with my Grandmama and Granddaddy. The following are my favorite memories of Grandmamma and Granddaddy.

When we ate a meal, Granddaddy would sit at the head of the table. My usual place was to the left of Granddaddy, and Grandmama would be to his right. I would get a kick out of reaching over and twisting the hairs on his arm! After all, *he* was the one that taught most of us to joke and have a sense of humor. He was quite the influence! One of his favorite things to eat for breakfast was Grandmama's biscuits, but not just a plain ole' biscuit. He would pour Karo and Blackburn syrup on his plate, mix in a large spoonful of peanut butter and dip a biscuit into it! Sometimes, Grandmama would burn the biscuits, and after she would sit them on the table, he would say, "Look, they have chocolate on the bottom!" Oh, my goodness, these meals would have to be some of the funniest and most memorable times with him! He would tease me and others so much. A certain few of my cousins said they were going to write down his different jokes and sayings since there were so many!

Granddaddy used to say to me, "Is that your dog behind you?" There wouldn't be a dog there, but he thought it was funny to make me look. One time, he said that to me, and there actually *was* a dog behind me! If any of the grandkids fell and didn't get hurt, he would say, "I didn't see you, do it again!" When I was old enough to have a boyfriend, and he saw me walking hand-in-hand with them, he would say, "Tammy, if you let go, I'll help you catch him!" Let me tell you, they broke the mold when they made Granddaddy, and I have never met another person like him in my entire life.

Teasing wasn't one-sided with Granddaddy. You could tease him, too, and he didn't mind being on the receiving end of a good joke. One of the things that the entire family liked to tease Granddaddy about was that he watched the soap opera, *The Young and the Restless*! He always claimed that it was only Grandmama that watched it, but we all knew better. Any of us could walk in the room, and he could tell us exactly what was going on in the storyline at any given time.

Grandmama and Granddaddy spent a lot of time with Shaun and me because we lived with them quite a bit growing up. My grandparents saw

Jeremy quite a bit, too, because he lived nearby. Eventually, Gary, Chris, and Rebecca moved to Florida, so it was difficult to see them.

Grandmamma and Granddaddy would take the grandkids to Scott's Apple Orchard several times a year. We would usually get one bushel of Red Delicious apples, one bushel of Granny Smith apples, and some apple cider. We loved going to the orchard! One tradition that we always looked forward to all year long was Grandmama and Granddaddy driving us around Huntsville to look at Christmas lights during the holiday season.

Granddaddy enjoyed going to the local auction so that he could find "good deals." Now, we aren't talking about some fancy, highfalutin auction! This auction wasn't an auction for valuable art or classic cars. This auction was for *used* items that were still in good usable condition. Granddaddy did find some "good deals" for things he and Grandmama needed at home, but he also found quite a few toys for us at this auction. Many of the toys, particularly the riding toys that I grew up playing with at their house, came from the auction. We didn't care that they weren't brand new. I remember the time that he took my cousin, Gary, and me, to the auction. Granddaddy was quick to warn Gary not to raise his hand because he didn't want Gary to bid on something that he would then have to buy!

All of the grandkids would always have a blast playing together at my grandparent's house! I'm sure I could speak for all of us when I say that we spent some of the best times of our lives growing up at Grandmama and Granddaddy's house. There are so many great stories that I could share, but here are some of my favorite memories of those times with my cousins.

One of my favorite things to do was playing outside on a brand-new swing-set that Granddaddy bought for us! I would play on it for hours, especially with Shaun and Jeremy! We would play like we were *The Dukes of Hazzard*. I was Daisy, of course! Shaun and Jeremy would go as high as they could go on the part of the swing set that had the double swing. Jeremy would pretend to be Luke Duke because he has brown hair, and Shaun, having blonde hair, would pretend to be Bo Duke! We would all go as high as we could in those swings and then jump out of them. Of course, we had to yell, "Yee-Haw," like the Duke's would do when jumping the General Lee! Most of the time, we just loved playing outside. We especially loved all of the various riding toys that Granddaddy bought us over the years. We had tricycles, bicycles, big wheels, and even an old pogo stick! I think I just about wore out the green tricycle and red wagon that we had at my grandparents.

I will admit that I did go through a short-lived tomboy phase with my cousins and brother, where I would climb trees and occasionally even get on the roof of the house, though I am terrified of heights. We didn't do this too often, but we would play in the dirt and mud with some of Grandmama's older pots and pans! Catching lightning bugs at night was another thing I enjoyed doing during my tomboy phase. I would take an old pickle jar, poke holes in the lid, and then go outside to collect as many lightning bugs as I possibly could in the evenings. I would keep the lightning bugs I caught in my room, but unfortunately, the lighting bugs usually didn't survive the night.

Another thing that I was into during this "phase" was watching wrestling on TV! My favorite wrestlers were Hulk Hogan, André the Giant, George "The Animal" Steel, Junkyard Dog, The British Bulldogs, Randy "Macho Man" Savage, and of course, Miss Elizabeth! I'm not sure how my short-lived obsession with wresting started, but I do remember arguing with Granddaddy *several* times that wrestling was, in fact, *real*! I refused to accept the possibility that it *may* not be real!

Sometimes, we would play in Granddaddy's camper that he stored in the backyard, on a tire swing that he hung from a tree, or even our parents old Croquet set that my grandparents had kept for years at their house. One time, Gary and I came up with the idea to teach football lessons in the front yard. We even posted advertising signs! No one came, but Gary did teach *me* how to throw a spiral! Gary and I also planted some actual pieces of yellow corn in my grandparent's garden, just to see what would happen. Something happened, alright, but it wasn't much! Some green sprouts, probably weeds, started coming up out of the ground later, but they weren't corn stalks!

If we were playing inside, we loved to play "store." The local grocery stores would bag your groceries in these big brown paper sacks, and Grandmama always had these around the house. We would pretend to buy and sell things in Grandmama's house and use the paper sacks to carry everything. Grandmama didn't care, as long as we put everything back where we found it! We would also use these sacks to make masks by cutting out places for your eyeballs and drawing noses and lips on them. We could find ways to entertain ourselves with almost anything. We would also play our version of the famous *Bozo Grand Prize Game* that we watched on WGN, out of Chicago. Another game we would play inside was "The Quiet Game." I'm quite sure that my grandparents enjoyed us playing this, more than we did! Usually, it seemed that either Gary or Chris would eventually do something funny to make the rest of us laugh so that we would lose the game!

Gary and I would pretend we were news anchors delivering the nightly news. We were both so young that I'm not sure if he recalls us doing this or not. I would start with a news segment or two, and when it was his turn, I'd say, "Back to you, Gary!" He would then give his portion of the news. We would just keep going back and forth, making up news stories and giggling.

One evening, Granddaddy was watching all of the grandkids. I only remember him watching *all* of us this one time. When I say "watching us," I mean he was sleeping, and we did whatever we wanted. Except for one thing, our parents left us with one chore to do while they and Grandmama were gone. We had to wash the dishes! We came up with this bright idea on how we could get the job done faster since there were so many dishes. We started an assembly line! We laid towels, end-to-end, on the floor that stretched from the kitchen sink to one of the back bathrooms in the house. While some of us washed the dishes at the kitchen sink, some would walk them on the towels to the bathroom for rinsing in that sink, and then back to dry off and put away. We were so smart! Mission accomplished, and Granddaddy slept through the whole thing!

Grandmama and Granddaddy would often take us to southern Alabama to visit both sides of the family. I loved going to see my Great Grandmama Taylor, Granddaddy's mother. She always baked a cake and had it ready to eat when we arrived. It was usually a red velvet cake, which is still one of my favorites! During our visits, we would sometimes go to the library that was next door to her house. When it was time for us to go home, she would always cry, as she waved goodbye to us. I consider myself fortunate to have two cobalt blue "genie bottle" decanters that were passed down to me from her displayed in my house. The decanters are antiques and much older than I am!

We would also go to visit Granddaddy's aunt and uncle that had a farm. I loved going there, as well. My Uncle Chester would take us for rides on the tractor, and we helped feed the chickens. They had a giant front porch swing that I loved to swing on. There were train tracks directly across the road from the farmhouse. Mom told us that when she and her siblings were growing up, they would sit on the front porch, wave at the passing trains, and motion for the train engineer to blow the horn for them. I was used to eating the "white" store-bought eggs, and remember, I did not like having to eat the "brown" eggs! The brown eggs tasted "funny" to me, considering I was a city girl! I didn't know at the time that the difference was because they were fresh eggs! Aunt Allie always seemed to wear similar dresses and would do all of her farm work in them. Uncle Chester would always wear overalls. I would play in the outdoor sink that was on the back porch. It was supposed to be used to clean yourself up before going inside the house and always had a bar of soap on it. My aunt and uncle never had any children of their own, but they sure loved it when we came to visit! I was not used to the country life, but I'll tell you what, I could sit on the front porch and shell peas as good as anyone! Oh, but don't drop that pan, as there would be enough peas to pick up for days!

Years later, Grandmama and Granddaddy would inherit this farm. Although at the time they inherited it, it was no longer a working farm. The property had the old white farmhouse and a large red barn on about 100 acres. My Granddaddy would sometimes sell pecans from the pecan trees in the front yard because they were a popular item that the locals in the area would use for baking cakes and pies. Granddaddy gave me my great-great Aunt Allie's China set, from the 1930s, and I have it proudly displayed in my home.

As you can see, I certainly experienced many ups and downs during this time in my life. While there were many great and beautiful memories, there was also much change, confusion, and pain. I longed for stability, but these years would only be a precursor of the events to follow.

Chapter 4

The Awkward Middle

Mom, Shaun, and I temporarily moved out of my grandparent's home and into a rental house on the other side of town. My relationship with Mom began taking a turn for the worse when we moved out. I would still try to get my mom's attention, especially if she had a boyfriend visiting. I began confronting her about her behaviors that I didn't like. The friction continued to grow between us, due to the negative interactions we would have during my middle school years. These interactions were shaping how I viewed myself, my mom, and our relationship. Keep in mind that if I were eleven or twelve at this time, Mom would have only been in her late twenties. She was working full-time and raising two kids, one with Cerebral Palsy, without any help from each of our fathers. Fortunately, she did receive support from Grandmama and Granddaddy. Of course, I was too young to comprehend the complexity of everything going on at the time, and it would be years before I could fully understand.

One of the most vivid memories during this time happened while I was sitting at our dining room table reading my Bible. Mom walked into the room, and without me saying a word to her, she looked at me and said, "Oh, give me a break!" It made me feel so hurt, rejected, and ashamed when she said this to me.

I was now old enough to recognize when Mom would have men over for part of the night before leaving. I began confronting her about these things. I resented her for it and was becoming more and more contemptuous. As the resentment grew inside of me, it began spilling out in unproductive ways.

During my birthday party at our home, I started choking. I don't recall what it was I was choking on, but I remember my mom's reaction. She started freaking out and acting as if she didn't even know what to do. My grandparents stepped in to help me when I started choking. Afterward, I called her out in front of my grandparents by yelling, "See, she doesn't even know what to do!" I'm sure I did this because of the bitterness and resentment I was beginning to develop toward her.

It seemed to me that my mom was continually criticizing me. I felt as if I couldn't do anything right in her eyes. All I ever wanted growing up was for her to pay more attention to me, to be proud of me, or at least, just not be embarrassed by me. I'm not saying that my mom was embarrassed by me, but I felt like I was an embarrassment to her. She would still get on to me for not getting all of the shampoo out of my hair and make me keep rinsing it until I got it right. I also started gaining a few pounds around this time. At Christmas, Mom bought me a sweatshirt, but she packed it inside the original box for a set of dumbbells. When I first saw the box and was confused before I opened it, she said, "Well, you said you wanted to lose some weight!" Whether she meant it to be hurtful at the time or not, this hurt my feelings.

Mom would be defensive toward me when I would confront her about her boyfriends. There was one specific time when she told me that she was going over to her boyfriend's house, and she was taking Shaun with her because "Shaun didn't judge her!" Well, Shaun would have only been around five or six at this time and had no idea what was going on. I recall this day vividly because I was so angry at her that I went to my room after she had left, took all of the ballerina jewelry boxes that she had gotten me, and destroyed all of them! I put them in trash bags and put them by the street. She either didn't notice or never let me know that she did.

It would have been around this time that I noticed some perfectionistic ways starting to show. I began to regularly clean, organize, or rearrange the furniture in my room. I may not have been able to control some things, but I was able to control other things to make me feel better. I did not want to live in this house with her. I felt better and safer living with my grandparents. I also felt that while we were living with my grandparents, I was happier. I believe they unknowingly helped control matters, to a certain degree, because there wasn't as much friction in their house, and my mom's demeanor was different.

During these days, I was extraordinarily nosy and felt like I had to know everything that was going on. I often worried and didn't want any surprises. My mother would point this out to me often, and she would make comments about me being a "worrywart" and that I was always in everyone's business.

I desperately desired to get Mom's attention. One time, in an attempt to get it, I ran away from home. It wasn't for very long. It wasn't even for a day or even several hours, but when I came back home, she didn't even know that I had "run away." I had only gone down the street and stayed there for a while. I didn't know what I had to do to get her attention. Whether *earning* it through behaving myself or *forcing* it through acting out, nothing I tried was getting me what I felt I needed. I needed to feel accepted, and my feelings validated by the most important person in my life, my mom. She was supposed to be my role model.

We eventually moved back in with my grandparents. Mom worked from 7:00 am to 3:30 pm, Monday through Friday. However, she was not home most nights. She would say she was "going out." For years, she was hanging out with the wrong crowd. These people were her coworkers, and they were not a good influence. I resented her for it. I wanted her *to want* to be with me, and I felt *less important* than her coworkers.

At one point, Mom rented an apartment just around the corner from my grandparent's house. I made it known to my mom and my grandparents that I didn't want to live with her. I didn't want to live with her because I felt that her behavior had not changed, especially as it pertained to her lifestyle. At first, I didn't have to go, but eventually, Mom made me move back in with her. While I was living with my grandparents, I realized how much I liked having a separate bedroom and not having to share one with Shaun, and how much I enjoyed not being around the lifestyle that Mom was living.

My fears about her lifestyle were confirmed. On the very first night that I was back with Mom, she snuck someone into her room. I had been waiting up to see if something like this would happen. Well, it did, and we got into an argument the next day because I called her out on it. I found out that it had been one of her former boyfriends that I had issues with previously. It wasn't too long before we had to move back in with my grandparents. Years later, I asked my mother about all these times, and she explained to me that she just wanted to be loved. Mom admitted to me that she knew that there were times that she was not there for me and could have done a better job. As a pre-teen, however, there is no way that I *could* have or *should* have been expected to comprehend these things on either an intellectual level or an emotional level.

I would get so upset and angry at some of the ways my mom would treat me. One morning, I remember that when she got mad at me, she refused to let me borrow "her" hair gel to get ready for school. At the time this happened, my hair was wavy and could be unruly. I was embarrassed about having to go to school looking this way. I felt like my mom knew this and is why she did what she did to me that morning. When we would have these types of arguments at home, I would go to school feeling like an emotional wreck and not be able to concentrate on school. I recall talking to a friend in class about some of these problems I was having at home.

In the eighth grade, she was mad at me on my birthday. I went to class devastated and crying because she didn't tell me "Happy Birthday" before dropping me off at school. I was old enough to know that I shouldn't be treated this way, and I resented her for it. I honestly did despise her at times growing up, as awful as it sounds. I can't remember if it was for her birthday or Christmas, but I wanted to get her something special, and I didn't have any money. I decided that I would go through everything that I had and give her some of my nicest things. I gathered up items, like a pair of newer earrings, and placed them in a light-brown oval wicker basket. Instead of her being grateful, she criticized me! In so many words, she reminded me that these particular occasions come around every year and that I could have planned better if I wanted to get her something nice. This event would be a defining moment for me! I felt so much shame and not good enough for her.

I have great memories of the times that we celebrated Christmas at my grandparents growing up. Grandmama would bring home real candy canes from her work. We hung them on the Christmas tree and ate the left-overs that we didn't use on the tree. However, I didn't like this one ornament that Grandmama had on their Christmas tree. It was a bird ornament that made a loud, obnoxious chirping noise!

If I thought elementary school was rough, middle school taught me just how mean and cruel kids could be to other kids! During my middle school years, I didn't like myself. I was super nerdy, and at times, overweight. I didn't know how to style my hair or apply makeup. One day, my mother noticed some hair growing under my arms and criticized me by telling me that I needed to start shaving. She said it in a manner that caused me to feel humiliated. I didn't know any better. Some of my school clothes were hand-me-downs, but occasionally I would get something new.

In sixth grade, there was a girl in my English class that always felt the need to hit me. I don't know why she hit me, but I was afraid of her and didn't want to get in trouble. She would usually do this when the teacher left the classroom. Looking back, I wish I would have stood up for myself. I loathed her and what she did to me. On a good note, there was a boy named Danny in my homeroom that liked me. I had a small Cabbage Patch Kids memo pad that had my name and phone number in it that I used in class. I left it in class one day, because the next thing I knew, Danny was calling me on the phone. Two years later, we would dance together at an eighth-grade dance and kiss. Mom walked me to class on the first day of school, up through the 6th grade. Most parents didn't do this, and I remember that it made me feel special.

A certain few girls would make fun of me and other girls at school, especially in P.E. I would be made fun of because I had purple tennis shoes with Velcro on them, and not the name-brand Reeboks that these girls wore. My mom couldn't afford name-brand shoes for me at the time. These things were happening at school during the time that we were alternating living with or separately from Grandmama and Granddaddy. During one of the times that I was living with my grandparents by myself, Grandmama had promised that she would take me to buy some new tennis shoes. I don't remember everything that was said, but I do remember lashing out at both Grandmama and Granddaddy for not taking me. I was so tired of the kids at school making fun of me, and I was taking my frustrations out on them.

I often heard the words come out of my mom's mouth, "We can't afford it." I tried out for and made the middle school track team, but Mom couldn't afford the running shoes that I was supposed to wear. The school allowed me, along with another girl in the same situation, to wear our regular shoes. I wanted to try out for cheerleading, not that I would have likely made the squad, but it didn't matter because I knew we couldn't afford the uniforms. I wanted to play soccer, and Mom let me sign up. I felt different because I didn't have everything the other kids had on my team. Upon arriving for one of my soccer practices, Mom and I had an argument because I wasn't dressed like the other kids. We went home, and I don't recall ever going back after this argument. When I did participate in activities, I remember feeling like Mom didn't want to be at the events. My impression was that she felt they were a nuisance and burdensome to her. Therefore, *I* was a nuisance and burdensome to her. I don't know if this is true on her part, but it is how I felt at the time.

I now know that this was not my mom's fault, but when I was in middle school, I couldn't fully understand her situation. We just couldn't afford these things. All I realized at the time was that I saw that the kids that had money seemed to have a more comfortable and better life that was mostly free from ridicule. Mom later bought me a pair of Reeboks, and the kids didn't make fun of me anymore. Special occasions, such as a school dance, were an exception. Mom usually found a way to buy me a new outfit. I still remember that for one dance, Mom bought me a shirt that had a white background with colorful patterns on it. To go with it, she also bought me a red belt that hung off my hips (it was supposed to) and red heart earrings, which made me feel special.

I enjoyed being a member of the choir in middle school and loved our choir teacher! I was an alto and could sing very well. My childhood friend, Susan, who lived around the corner from my grandparents, was also in the choir. Unfortunately, I couldn't even escape bullies in my choir class! There was a boy that made fun of my eyes. He called me "bug eyes," which hurt my feelings. I knew my eyes were huge, but what I didn't realize at the time was that later on in life, my eyes would be one of my best assets. My eyes are the feature that I get the most compliments on now. It's amazing to me how certain things turn around for the better in due time! Our school choir was selected to participate in the All-City choir. Mom was able to attend our All-City performance at the Civic Center. I remember seeing Granddaddy there, which surprised me because I wasn't expecting him. What surprised me, even more, was the fact that when he showed up to greet Mom and me, he was with another woman. There will be more on this later, though I didn't realize it at the time. Grandmama wasn't able to attend because she had to work.

I had to watch Shaun and Jeremy after I got out of school every afternoon because all of the adults were still at work. I was petrified to go into my grandparent's empty house and to stay by myself, at least until Shaun and Jeremy arrived from their school. They were still in elementary school and would walk to Grandmama and Granddaddy's every day together. I would always enter their house through the den door. Granddaddy had enclosed the carport and converted it into a den. I would always stay in the den and sit on the arm of the couch until the boys arrived. I wouldn't go anywhere else in the house. I don't know why I was so afraid to stay by myself or what I was so afraid would happen. I was so angry and resentful that I had to watch Shaun and Jeremy every day after school because I wasn't able to go over to my friend's houses to play after school. I became so angry that I would sometimes take it out on Jeremy and Shaun. I would make them stand in the corner, and I was physically abusive toward them, at times. I deeply regret mistreating them in this way. I wanted to be like most of my friends and do what they got to do. Of course, in my mind, it was *all* my mom's fault, so here again, I was taking my frustrations out on those closest to me.

It was in the seventh grade that I met Tammy Smith. Tammy would go on to be my best friend from the time I was twelve, until today. I am forty-six now, so that is an awfully long time. I am so grateful for our friendship.

Mom and Tammy's parents would take turns taking us to the skating rink on the weekends. Tammy and I loved to go to the skating rink! We loved roller-skating and talking about the "hot" boys that were there! We looked forward to seeing them in the "Trucking Skating Contests" every weekend. Over time, Tammy and I became outstanding skaters, and I began entering the skating contests. My team always did well, and occasionally we would win a contest!

I would usually spend the night at Tammy's house after going skating. I loved that her mom would make us Campbell's SpaghettiOs or Chef Boyardee Ravioli! I remember being slightly envious of Tammy because she always had things like Reeboks and Coca-Cola shirts that were popular at the time. I appreciated that she would let me borrow them sometimes. Although they would not have been considered wealthy, Tammy differed from me in that both of her parents worked at the time. When I got a little older, Mom would occasionally let me borrow a few of her shirts to wear to school.

It was also in the seventh grade when I started my menstrual cycle. I recall that when this happened, my mom handled it very well. Mom told me that when she started her period, Grandmama didn't talk about these things with her. Grandmama just gave her a hug and some feminine pads. Mom said that she wanted to explain everything to me and wished that Grandmama would have talked to her about these types of things when she was growing up. I've always been thankful and appreciated this about Mom.

I am not exactly sure when I saw Alan for the last time, but I know the circumstances that led up to it. In addition to his disturbing kissing games, as I got older, he started to take things a bit further. When I started developing, he would encourage me to undress in front of him entirely. I would do as he said, but I would cover up my breasts. I insisted that I could run my bathwater, but Alan kept persisting that he would do it for me. After one of our visits, I went home and told my mom that I didn't want to go anymore when he came to pick up Shaun for future visits. Alan supposedly didn't understand why I didn't want to stay with him anymore, and I don't remember seeing him again after I told Mom what was happening to me.

During my middle school years, and as I spent more time with Mawmaw, I would begin to learn more about the family system, drinking, infidelity, gambling, and the abuse that happened on that side of my family. As a young girl, I overheard conversations that Mawmaw would have with others about Papa Karl. One day, Mawmaw took me in the car with her to an apartment complex. Before we got out of the car, Mawmaw said, "Now, we are going to go up and knock on a door. When the lady answers, you hurry and move out of the way!" I agreed. We walked up to the door, I knocked, and sure enough, a lady answered. Mawmaw quickly moved to the spot where I had been standing, as I stepped out of the way. As Mawmaw forced herself into the apartment, I was left standing outside by myself. The door was closed, so I had no idea what was going on inside. It seemed like Mawmaw was inside for a long time, but I'm sure it was only a few minutes before she came back outside. Mawmaw took me back to her car, and when we got into the car, Mawmaw explained to me that she had caught Papa cheating on her with the woman! We waited in the car until we saw Papa come out a few minutes later. Mawmaw told me that Papa was embarrassed, but that he was *really* embarrassed because I was with her.

In addition to Mawmaw telling me bits and pieces of the abuse she was subjected to by Papa Karl, I saw the evidence firsthand. Mawmaw said to me that Papa Karl was upset that he had lost a significant bet and had thrown a phone at her. Her ear was utterly black and blue. I rarely saw Papa Karl, but when I did, he always treated me well. I just knew that I didn't like it that he sometimes treated my Mawmaw the way he did! Other times, when things were going well, I would hear about him taking Mawmaw on several fancy trips, including to the Bahamas, and buying her many pieces of jewelry.

My middle school years were awkward for many reasons. I felt lost and invisible, I couldn't seem to find my place anywhere, I desired to be accepted, and I was still searching for stability. My relationship with my mom was crumbling along with my self-esteem. My frustration and resentment toward her was growing and was spilling out as defiance and anger. Sometimes my anger was directed toward her, other times, it was directed toward others, but it was most damaging when I directed inward to myself. There were ominous signs to the destruction that lay ahead for me, but no one, not even myself, realized just how quickly I was reaching my boiling point.

Chapter 5

Tennessee Bound!

I was in the ninth grade at Butler High School, where my mom and dad had graduated. Several of my aunts, uncles, and their spouses graduated from there, as well. It wasn't exactly the best school, even back when my mom attended. I found myself in a very awkward place. I just didn't seem to fit in. It didn't help that my best friend, Tammy, and I began losing contact and were not as close as we were in middle school. She started attending a private school in the ninth grade and didn't go to Butler High School. I went toward the only place I thought I could fit in and be accepted, and that was with the wrong crowd. I only attended Butler High School for one semester. During that one semester of school, I lost my virginity, tried marijuana, started smoking, skipped school several times, and I was failing a few classes.

Mom and I were not getting along at all. I gave up my virginity "to get it over with" and from peer pressure. I was so freaked out about having sex for the first time, that I thought I would become pregnant like my mom. I was a worrier anyway. It would be one of the worst decisions I have ever made. I didn't even like the boy. I tried marijuana and skipped school for the same reasons. I was still coming out of my nerdy phase from middle school. I felt like an ugly duckling. I couldn't style my hair or do my makeup good enough, my clothes were far from stylish, and not to mention, I was on the free-lunch program that completely humiliated and embarrassed me to death. I was on it in middle school, but when you get to high school, you knew that the other kids would eventually figure it out. I had a friend that was also on the free-lunch program. We would lie and tell anyone that asked that our parents pre-paid our lunches for the year. Many times, I wouldn't eat lunch because I was so embarrassed. If I did eat, I would wait until there were no other kids in line before I got my lunch. When I didn't eat lunch, I would go outside to the "smoking area" where the "cool kids" hung out. It was there that some of the boys started to pay attention to me, and a few thought I was cute.

I met Holly at school, and we quickly became close friends. Not long after we met, Holly decided to drop out of high school, but it didn't affect our friendship. There were times that I would skip school to hang out with Holly. She soon introduced me to Jonathan, and he became my boyfriend for a short time. He was a couple of years older than me and had already been in trouble, including being arrested. I continued to make poor, self-sabotaging decisions. It was also during this first semester in high school that I told Granddaddy that I didn't want to live anymore. I had no plans to do anything further with those thoughts, but they were still there nonetheless. My family was concerned about me and the decisions I was making that were quickly leading me down the wrong path.

Unbeknownst to me, my mother had decided that I was going to move to Tennessee with my Aunt Dianne and Uncle Jesse. The plan was for me to move to Collierville, Tennessee, for one year, and then I would move back home. I was in complete shock! I am not sure why I was shocked, as I was headed in an awful direction. I remember calling Mawmaw and her not understanding why I had to move. I remember being so angry at Mom. I questioned whether she was sending me to Tennessee because it was in my best interest or if it was because she didn't want to deal with me anymore. Anxiety consumed me concerning the move. I did not want to be separated from my brother, grandparents, and all of my friends. The next thing I knew, I was traveling down the roads between Huntsville and Collierville. I didn't know what lay ahead, but I knew I didn't want to leave my life, as I knew it, behind.

Not long after I arrived at my Aunt Dianne and Uncle Jesse's home, I was sitting alone in my bedroom that I shared with my cousin, Rebecca, crying my eyes out. I had so many thoughts going through my mind. "How can this be?" "Why was I even here?" I had just finished listening to a cassette tape that my friend, Holly, had mailed me. She was upset to the point of crying herself while telling me how much she missed me. I was devastated, but I wouldn't be for long.

I didn't have many personal items to bring with me from Huntsville, but I certainly brought a few bad habits. I kept my cigarettes in a yellow travel soap-box container hidden in my dresser drawer. I found the "cool" crowd at Collierville High School rather quickly and would occasionally join the girls in the bathroom for a quick smoke. Sometimes, when there was a dance or other after-school activity, I would bring a roll of quarters with me and call Jonathan using the payphone in the gym. It would usually cost $10 or more to call him on the payphone because it was considered a long-distance phone call at the time. I would soon have a talk with my family regarding the fact that the kids from Alabama that I thought were my friends were not honestly my friends. My family felt that I should drop my "friends" cold turkey because they didn't have my best interests at heart. Of course, they were not referring to my best friend, Tammy. Tammy and I had never gotten into trouble together, at least not yet anyway!

I eventually got settled in with my aunt, uncle, and cousins. Gary and I were both freshmen in high school. Chris and Rebecca were a few years behind us in school. I was ecstatic that Gary was not only in the same school as me but in the same grade! At least I wasn't alone! Gary did his best to make me feel comfortable and help with my transition to a new high school. Gary even took up for me when a girl was trying to bully me. Gary invited me to sit at the lunchroom table with him and his friends. I did a few times, and I understood what he was trying to do. I appreciated him protecting me and offering to include me, so I wouldn't feel like I didn't fit in. However, I wanted to make friends of my own and sit with them at lunchtime.

Initially, it was hard to fit in because Collierville was a small town, and most of the kids had grown up together. They had already formed their cliques, and I was the new kid from Alabama. If the social aspects of transitioning to a new high school midway through your freshman year weren't challenging enough, Collierville High School was also more academically challenging. The credits required for graduation were different, and the grading system was more strict than at Butler High School. I had to attend summer school to catch up! Eventually, I made it through and passed my courses, but I was angry and thought it was unfair that I had to even be in summer school. I didn't like most of the kids I was in class with that summer, and I got into a physical fight with a girl that kept getting on my nerves! I was resentful because I wasn't able to do what I wanted over the summer!

I began attending church after I moved to Collierville. We attended Greenhills Baptist Church. It was there that I met Connie and Cassandra, and they are still two of my best friends today! Connie went to high school with me but was a year ahead of me. Cassandra was homeschooled and was our pastor's daughter. About a year after I moved to Collierville, I met Sandy. She had just moved in with her aunt and family in Collierville, and we went to the same high school and church. Sandy also came from a troubled past, and she quickly became one of my best friends.

I am not sure why I acted this way, but often I would not come out of my bedroom or go anywhere. I would stay in my bedroom and watch TV. Eventually, I would stop doing this after I started making friends and going to church. Outside of having to attend summer school, I liked Collierville High School and my teachers. Initially, the other kids were standoffish, but over time, that changed, and most of them became accepting of me. Things were starting to turn around for me.

I accepted Jesus Christ as my Savior, was baptized, and I started to become very involved in church. My cousins and I would go to church camp, and one summer, I assisted in Vacation Bible School with the 3-year-old class. I would regularly attend Sunday services and remember listening about some of the various mission trips our church was involved in or supported. I enjoyed my Sunday school class and would do my best to answer my teacher's questions. My Sunday school teacher also happened to be our youth choir director. I participated in the church youth choir and performed a solo once during a worship service. My aunt and uncle would occasionally open up their home to hold youth activities.

The first time I ever rode a horse was when I went horseback riding with the youth at church. I was riding a horse named Patches and was at the back of the line of horses and riders. Patches decided *she* wanted to sprint to the front of the line of horses and even ran into the back end of another horse! I began freaking out because it was all I could do to hold on and not fall off. I went horseback riding one more time and decided to "hang up the reins." Everyone in my life was making me feel welcome. It was the first time I truly felt this much stability in my life and a part of a real family!

Before I moved in, Gary and Chris shared a bedroom, and Rebecca had her bedroom to herself. When I arrived, Rebecca had to share her room with me. She even had to share her bed with me for a short time until my aunt and uncle bought us separate twin-sized beds. I can't imagine what it was like for her to have me move in and her having to share her room, walk-in closet, and especially, her bed. It must have been a huge adjustment for her and the entire family as a whole! A year went by, and I thought I was going home, but I didn't. The decision was made by Mom, Aunt Dianne, and Uncle Jesse that since I was doing so well, that I would stay there longer. I was angry and disappointed at first, but not for long.

Rebecca and I would occasionally argue and bicker. I'm sure we were behaving in the same way that two sisters would act toward each other. I remember one argument was when I decided that I wanted to redecorate her

Barbie dollhouse, and it wasn't because I did a poor job. It was because I had not asked her permission! Oh, she wasn't going to tolerate it! She was infuriated and put it right back the way she originally had it set up. Something else that I remember about her Barbie dollhouse is that Rebecca had the idea to use a few of the white plastic dividers that are placed in the center of your pizza to keep the box from touching it as "end tables." I always thought that was such a smart idea!

The days of listening to Metallica and other heavy metal groups were supposedly over after I became a Christian. I say "supposedly" because we still listened to that type of music, and the lyrics weren't exactly Christian. Rebecca and I were allowed to have New Kids on the Block posters in our bedroom! We had those cute boys hanging on the door of our walk-in closet. Jesse made us separate vanities for us to do our hair and makeup. We loved having our own space to get ready!

I liked that my aunt was able to stay at home, although she would occasionally work outside the home. She was always available to be there for us. It could be something as simple as cookies after school or being free to take us places we needed to go. To me, it was very comforting to know that someone was there for us. At home, we had various chores and responsibilities. We were assigned cooking nights and dish duty nights. Some of my aunt's favorite stories to tell about me was when I would try to cook. I guess I gave her plenty of material since I didn't know anything about cooking. One of her favorite stories was when a recipe called for "mixing by hand." I took it in the literal sense because I mixed everything with my *actual* hands! I'm a much better cook now, but I still don't like to cook much today.

As they say, "There was nothing any of us could have wanted for." Dianne and Jesse took great care of us and ensured that we always had anything we truly needed, and more, as they were able. They took me to the dentist for the *first* time in my life when I was sixteen, and later on, to have my wisdom teeth removed! Amazingly enough, I didn't have any cavities! As a teenager, I began focusing more on my outer appearance. One thing that bothered me about my appearance was my front teeth when I would smile. I remember telling Jesse that the way two of my front teeth looked bothered me. He didn't share my opinion, but he said that he understood why they bothered me.

I have so many great memories of the time I spent with my aunt, uncle, and cousins. My aunt and uncle treated me as if I were their child. Both of them taught me and guided me through these years. The following are a few of my most vivid memories while I stayed with them.

Dianne and I would often go walking around our neighborhood and talk. Those were special times that we spent together talking about anything and everything. A few times, Jesse took Gary and I up to his work. We would have so much fun playing video games while staying there all night. Jesse also took us roller-skating and even got on skates himself one time. I thought that was cool that he'd do that with us.

Rebecca and I had so many fun times together. One time, we were both riding a four-wheeler on the city streets in our neighborhood. We got pulled over by a local police officer, Officer Holt. You could tell when he pulled us over that he was trying not to smile, even laugh, too much. However, as soon as I knew who he was, I said, "Oh, you're Grant's daddy!" I said this knowing full well that I wasn't even friends with Grant, but knew that Gary was, and was trying to smooth things over. Officer Holt's face lit up with a smile, and he said, "Oh, you know my son?" To which I replied, "Yes, I go to school with him." After a short discussion that we shouldn't be riding our four-wheeler on the street, he let us off with a warning and sent us back home. I had a conversation with Rebecca a couple of years ago, and she shared with me that she had always viewed me as a sister. I knew that we were close while I lived with Dianne and Jesse, but I never realized that she thought of me as a sister. It was a special moment, and I will always remember that conversation.

Curiosity always seemed to get the best of us, whether it was Christmas or birthdays. One Christmas, we unwrapped and re-wrapped the presents and put them back under the tree. I believe that one year, my aunt and uncle hid the gifts in the trunk of their car to keep us from finding out what they bought us! One of the best gifts that we ever received when our family got our first computer. It was the best thing ever! One of our favorite things to do was to play games on the computer, and my personal favorite was *Wheel of Fortune*.

I had always wanted a dog, more specifically, a Collie. As a surprise one day, not long after I found out that I was going to continue living with Dianne and Jesse, they took me to Jesse's work. There was a little puppy cocker spaniel, and she was mine! She may not have been a Collie, but she was so cute! She was a sandy color, so that is what I named her! We set up a baby gate for Sandy in the kitchen. She would climb up one side of the gate and fall to the floor on the other side. While she was able to figure out how to escape the kitchen, she didn't seem to be the brightest dog in all areas. We had a glass kitchen table and when there was food on top of the table, Sandy would jump up and hit her head on the glass. She *never* learned that she couldn't get to the food through the glass tabletop. She would also slightly pee now and then when you picked her up. Although this usually is not a good thing, it did come in handy sometimes when I had to take her outside to do her business. If she were taking too long, I would hold Sandy up while walking her on the grass, in hopes that she would go pee quickly!

When I was sixteen, I wanted a job to make some money. My first job was at Baskin-Robbins. All of my coworkers went to my school, and my friend, Cassandra, also started working there with me. It was a great job, and I experienced some of the best times of my life while working there. My friends would come in after school and *try* to get extra toppings, of course! I quickly found out that if pineapple sits for a while, it ferments! We used these enormous metal scoopers to scoop out the ice-cream. All of us swore that our scooping arm muscles were disproportionally larger than our non-scooping arm! Something else that I learned is that you don't know what cold is until you continuously walk in-and-out of a huge walk-in freezer! Every shift we worked, we got two free scoops of ice-cream. Is there anything better than free ice-cream?

I remember thinking how lucky we were to work at Baskin-Robbins. Most kids were working in fast-food, while we were making sundaes and waffle cones! Part of my training was learning how to make everything on the menu! We had to practice, but couldn't sell my lop-sided banana splits, so I would occasionally call my family to come and get the desserts we couldn't sell. They certainly didn't complain about eating lop-sided banana splits! There were times that my aunt or other family members would bring me something to eat at work. I remember them commenting on some of my odd requests. They were like, "Who in the world asks to be brought turnip greens for lunch?" They weren't cooked at home, as I was about the only person that ate them! I grew up eating all of the "southern-country" food that Grandmama and Granddaddy ate. I was from a very "country" family on both sides, but some of them have told me that I am "different," I guess what they were saying is that I'm as country as a city girl can be! I eventually became a manager and keyholder at my job. I worked at Baskin-Robbins during my last two years of high school.

I loved being able to work and earn money. I would usually buy clothes with the money I earned. Over time, I began to acquire the types of clothes that were popular with kids my age that I had always desired to own. We were required to make our beds every day, and I kept my room super clean! My family and friends would joke with me because of my closet. I would organize my clothes and rotate them on the rod so I wouldn't wear the same set of clothing within two weeks of each other! I suppose this was part of my OCD ways. I would wear dresses at church and occasionally wear them to school. I was becoming quite the girly-girl! Not all of my outfits were store-bought. One of my favorites was a red jumpsuit that had a black top underneath it and a black tie-belt to match that Dianne had sewn for me. I was proud of this outfit and wore it a lot.

When I turned sixteen, I was not in a hurry to get my driver's license. For some reason, I was afraid to drive. Dianne and Jesse had to make me get my license when I was seventeen! I also found out that I was required to have glasses because I couldn't see well enough to drive at night. Unrelated to my driving at night, I have always been afraid of the dark. Even now, to a certain degree, I'm still scared of the dark. That's a pretty hard pill to swallow, but it's true. I slept with the bathroom light on until I was fifteen years old! One night, I had to get something out of a vehicle in the driveway, and my uncle Jesse and I had a quick conversation about me being fearful of the dark. I don't recall the details of the conversation, but I still remember feeling afraid. I can't quite explain some of my fears or why they exist, but I am just not comfortable with the darkness.

My uncle Jesse taught me many things while I stayed with them. One of the most significant for me was when he told me, "If you don't stand up for yourself, no one else will!" I wanted to try out for cheerleading, but I didn't have enough credits. It was due to me transferring from Alabama. Jesse went up to the school and fought for me to be able to try out. I appreciated him doing this for me and being a good example! Well, he convinced the administration to let me try out. I didn't make the squad, but I learned a great life lesson. I wasn't big on speaking up for myself at this time in my life and was still quite shy and timid in some ways. Early on, before I started making friends, I would avoid going to the large lunchroom and sitting down with kids I didn't know. It was very intimidating to me! No one else knew this, but many times, I would take my food from the lunchroom and walk to another part of the building to eat. There would be times that I would quietly eat my lunch in a bathroom stall, just to be away from other people. I remember thinking this was one of the loneliest feelings in the world, yet I was too ashamed to admit to anyone what I had been doing. I did this until I started to make friends and became comfortable enough to eat with them in the lunchroom.

Just like when I was younger, I loved art class. It was my favorite class in high school. I also enjoyed taking my Housing and Interiors and Child Development vocational classes. My favorite subjects were business-related, such as Business Math, Business Law, Office Skills (typing), and Accounting. I will never forget the time that my Office Skills teacher had an idea to boost up some of the students in the class. She gave everyone in the class a small Styrofoam cup and had us write our name on it. Our assignment was to think of a positive characteristic or trait about each of the other students in the class, write it down on a piece of paper, fold it up, and place it in their cup. It made many of us feel valued and appreciated! I loved reading the kind things people had to say about me, even if it was something simple like I had a beautiful smile or nice hair!

Speaking of my hair, I had long, thick, curly hair! Whew, it was a hot mess! Eventually, I got it all chopped off, and I'm talking short! In high school, many girls wore a popular short hairstyle that had a weight-line in the back and shaved under and slightly on the sides above your ears. I would continue to have a short hairstyle for many years. Bless Dianne's heart! One time, she tried to do both Gary and my hair at home. She attempted to give Gary a weight-line cut and give me blonde highlights. Neither of these two looks turned out as well as we would have hoped, but we could both still be seen in public and appreciated her efforts nonetheless!

Dianne and Jesse allowed Gary and me to hold a dance in the backyard. We put up lights, and Dianne helped make the food. Unfortunately, it was a bust! Only a few kids from our high school showed up, but we still had a great time anyway!

Gary and I were required to hold back 10 percent of our paychecks and give it Dianne and Jesse to teach us to be financially responsible with our income. Later, they returned this money to us for whatever we needed, following graduation. We also had to pay for all of our gas and a portion of our car insurance. Jesse and Dianne purchased us a maroon 1981 T-top Camaro for us to share, but occasionally, we would use Jesse's truck. Gary and I had so much fun and did some crazy things in that car. One time, we squeezed eight people in the car, with the T-tops off. Another time, we were driving near our high school and came across a stretch of highway that was under construction. The construction crews had placed several orange construction cones down the middle of the road. Being ornery teenagers,

Gary and I thought it would be funny to pick up a few cones, place them in the car, and drop them off further down the road at the end of the construction zone.

One of my favorite things to do with Chris was to stay up late at night and watch comedy shows on TV. We would laugh so hard that we would cackle. Chris could be a little devil, at times, because of his practical jokes! It is *still* true today! One time, I was sitting under the hairdryer in the kitchen, getting ready for a school dance, and reading a magazine. Chris came by and snatched the magazine out of my hands. I just about had a come apart because he broke one of my nails. Another time, Chris had a bright idea to scare me. He hid in the clothes hamper in the bathroom because he knew I was about to go in the bathroom to get ready. As I was shutting the door, Chris popped out of the hamper. He just about got "popped" himself, because I wanted to beat the snot out of him for doing that to me!

Jesse taught each of us, even the girls, how to change a tire, check oil, and other maintenance things on a vehicle. He also taught us gun safety and how to shoot different types of firearms. I'm thankful that he took the time to do these essential things with us. Dianne taught me many things, as well. I remember Dianne patiently teaching me how to fill out my bank deposit slips because, for some reason, I just couldn't catch on quickly at the time!

We had a house fire when I was in high school and living in Collierville. We found out later that it was due to a fireplace insert. It happened three days after Christmas and was one of the most hurtful and devastating times of my entire life. We got through it as a family, and the outreach by our church and our small community was overwhelming! My jewelry box had melted shut, but I was able to crack it open and recover the jewelry. These pieces of jewelry were my only personal items that survived the fire. We managed to salvage a few pictures that were still hanging on a wall. They just so happened to be our family portraits from church! When Rebecca and I walked upstairs to our bedroom, our headboard frames were about the only recognizable things in our room! I had two fish in a fishbowl made out of a bubble gum machine. I had a white angelfish, Madonna, and a purple angelfish, Passion, which was a famous Elizabeth Taylor perfume at the time. They were both gone.

We temporarily moved into a rental house for four months while we built our new home on the same property. It was bigger and better than our previous one. Some of the significant improvements were that we were able to add an in-ground pool, each of the kids had a separate bedroom, and we now had new furniture throughout the home. Though it was a devastating time that we had just gone through with the fire and losing virtually everything we owned, things soon began to improve for us. One of the hardest parts that I can recall about the house fire, other than the obvious emotional toll, was having to list everything we owned for the insurance company. Think about that for a minute. Every single item you owned! What an incredible list it turned out to be! Jesse spoke with our school principals right after the fire because he was concerned for us and wanted to make sure that the teachers or students didn't say or do anything to make us feel uncomfortable. Again, the fire was a tragedy, but it was amazing to see the rally of support that was provided by our church and small community.

I only dated a little bit in high school. I had a couple of boyfriends, but they didn't last long. I went to Prom and a few of the school dances. One boyfriend, Ben, was a year older than me. We attended different churches and met when our youth groups participated in the same ice skating event. We started dating, and I was his date for Prom. I have an "it wasn't funny at the time" story about Ben. One time, Ben and I were parking, and a police officer pulled up and talked to us. I was so afraid that the police officer was going to contact Dianne and Jesse that I went home and "told" on myself. I first went to Dianne and told her what happened. She said I had to tell Jesse. I was so scared. Jesse tried as hard as he could, but he burst out laughing while I was telling him. I found out later that it was all Dianne could do to keep a straight face while I told her. In case you are wondering, the police officer never contacted Dianne and Jesse.

My friend, Sandy, moved back to Mississippi, where she was initially from to live with her mom. It made me sad when she left Collierville. One time, we were on our way to Huntsville to visit family, and we stopped by Sandy's house as we were passing through Mississippi. I later learned from someone in her family that she had returned to her former bad habits and that she had become pregnant. I was hurt and disappointed when I heard this because a couple of years prior, Sandy and I gave our testimonies in the church to a group of younger girls. We had stressed the importance to them of what paths not to go down in life.

I graduated from high school in 1992. Mom, Aunt Dianne, Uncle Jesse, and both sets of my grandparents attended my graduation. My original plan was to enroll in the Baptist School of Nursing in Memphis, Tennessee, following graduation. However, I made the decision that I would move back home with Mom and Shaun. I moved back the day following my graduation.

I remember feeling so torn between two families. Just before I left to move back to Huntsville, I was crying as I thanked my aunt and uncle for everything they had done for me. I asked how I could ever repay them. My uncle replied, "Just keep your head on straight."

Once I moved back to Huntsville, I enrolled in a local community college and started taking a few courses. I thought I wanted to have a career in nursing but quickly figured out that it wasn't a good fit for me. I wasn't sure exactly what I wanted to do, so I started working full-time. I met back up with my best friend, Tammy, and she soon introduced me to Kyle. She had dated Kyle for a short time, but it didn't work out. Kyle and I hit it off right from the start, and Tammy didn't mind that I was dating him.

Chapter 6

Bruised and Confused

Kyle was a few years older than me and lived just around the corner from my grandparents with his mom. He had attended a local trade school and worked as a machinist. We seemed to click well at first, and the attraction I had for him was strong. Kyle was an intense person, and he had a bad temper that wouldn't show right away. He could be a very jealous and protective person, as well. We dated on-again and off-again for three years. I was terrified of potentially becoming pregnant, so I ensured that I took my birth control pills regularly. I didn't drink much at this time, but I did begin smoking again, even though you are not supposed to smoke while on birth control pills. Having just graduated from high school, I was enjoying my new-found freedom and began to slip into some of my old habits gradually. I would attend church, but not regularly.

I recall being in an argument with Kyle on a night that I had a college class. I skipped the class to work things out with him. Looking back, I felt like I would do *anything* to be loved and receive attention from a guy. So much so, that I had low self-esteem and would put up with just about anything. When I became of legal drinking age, I started going out to bars and drinking more. Eventually, I dropped out of college. If I could go back in time and change things, I wouldn't have given up college for a guy!

Kyle would drive drunk with me in the car, sometimes getting up to 100 mph. When I look back on this, I'm profoundly disappointed in myself. At some point, while I was dating Kyle, I recall running into my dad, and ironically, he told me not to put up with that behavior. I assume that Mawmaw had told him about some of the things that were going on. My relationship with Mom was on-again, off-again. Even though our relationship wasn't the best, I was proud that she had gone to secretarial school and was actively pursuing ways to better herself financially. She seemed to be living a party lifestyle with her friends, and it was a very different life than I had just come from in Collierville.

The abuse from Kyle started verbally but became physical over time. I remember attending one of Shaun's baseball games and sitting with Mom. She noticed the handprint on my leg. She knew what it was from and who did it to me. One time, I even had to go to work with a neck brace on because he had put his hands on me. My mom would get upset and plead with me about breaking up with him. She feared that I would eventually be seriously hurt or killed by him. I remember one evening walking out to my car that was parked at my mother's apartment complex and saw his Mustang parked across the street in an empty parking lot. He was stalking me!

Kyle and his friends would go to strip clubs and thought it was okay to watch porn in his mom's living room when she was out of town. It wouldn't even phase them when I would walk in on them as they were watching it. Looking back, I don't see how or why I tolerated any of this behavior. Kyle's mom was good to me. She understood that I had a strained relationship with my mom and struggled to maintain it, even after high school. There were times that Kyle's mom bought clothes for me, and she would often cook us meals.

I began to realize that nothing had changed between Mom and me. We were falling back into the same conflict patterns that we had before I moved to Collierville, so I moved out of Mom's apartment and in with Kyle and his mom. Kyle's mom was unaware of the abuse. She didn't learn what was going on until my Aunt Dianne visited me one day, and she insisted that I pack my things, come with her, and leave Kyle. Kyle's mom cried when she found out what he was doing to me. Kyle stayed outside in his car while I packed my things and left with Dianne. He sat there and watched everything unfold. I wish I could tell you that I never looked back on the relationship and that I never saw him again, but this wouldn't be the case.

I moved back in with Mom, at least until we got into another argument. This time, I moved out for good. I was nineteen. I rented an apartment, but I had to find a roommate to cover my expenses. While staying in this apartment, I would have two different roommates, but they both ended up moving out to move in with their boyfriends. Speaking of boyfriends, Kyle and I reconciled and got back together. My job temporarily laid me off, so things were hard financially for me. Without a job or roommate to help make ends meet, I let Kyle move in.

I eventually got tired of the toxic relationship with Kyle. We broke up, and he moved out of my apartment, but he *still* had a key. One night I was sleeping, and since I was afraid to stay by myself, I slept with the light on in my bedroom. I woke up in the middle of the night to find Kyle sitting in the corner of my room on the floor and drunk. He was *watching* me sleep! It was one of the scariest times in my life and was before everyone had cell phones! However, I did have a landline phone on the floor in the hallway. I knew if I could coerce or sweet talk him into the hall, I might be able to get to the phone. I also knew that Kyle wasn't going to leave quietly. He was begging and pleading with me to take him back. I finally talked him into going down the hallway and into the living room.

Since Kyle was drunk, I knew I had an advantage over him. I was scared, but this time, not too afraid to protect myself. I kicked Kyle, "where it counts," and he fell to the floor. I tied Kyle up with the long, straight phone jack cord and called the police. A police officer that lived in an adjacent apartment complex overheard the call come through on his scanner. Unfortunately, Kyle got loose from the phone cord and left before the police officer arrived. He had gotten away for the moment, but he wasn't going to let me get away with doing that to him. Kyle got drunk again and called me. I didn't answer the phone, and he left a very detailed voicemail on my answering machine explaining how he was going to kill me. I called the police, met with the local magistrate, and obtained a warrant. The police arrested Kyle at his job. Finally, this relationship was over for good.

Not long after I ended my relationship with Kyle, I found a better job that provided me with more pay and a steady income. It allowed me to move into a brand-new apartment by myself, and to purchase a newer and more reliable car. I started dating again, but none of the relationships lasted more than a few dates. I am not sure if it was because of my relationship with Kyle, but more and more of my temper was coming out. I was beginning to have an "I'm going to hurt you before you hurt me" attitude. I would consistently have arguments with the people that I was dating, so for a while, I decided it would be best to stay single and focus on other areas of my life. I still had a strained relationship with Mom, and would often go for extended periods without talking to her.

I still longed to have my dad in my life. I was not around my dad much growing up, and usually only saw him when I was with Mawmaw. I can only recall two times in my entire childhood that I stayed overnight at his house. It was extremely awkward for both of us, and he acted like he didn't know what to do around me. I didn't realize the extent that his absence and our interactions, while I was growing up, had shaped and impacted me. Not having a relationship with him was affecting my other relationships, though I wouldn't recognize the connection until much later in life.

Most of my childhood, I felt invisible to him. One example of this was when I was a young girl, and Mawmaw and I went to visit my Aunt Wanda. Dad and his current girlfriend came over to visit while we were there. I was playing in the back yard, and his girlfriend came over to talk to me. It was very apparent that she didn't know my relation to him. I knew she didn't know, and this made me upset. So, I purposely used the phrase "my dad" in a sentence with her, and it shocked her beyond belief! Later on, she came up to me and told me that she confronted my dad about me being his daughter. She was very friendly, which made me feel like she was a better person than my dad! All I knew was that I wasn't going to let her leave without her knowing that I was his daughter!

Earlier, I had told you that I have a half-sister, Amanda, from one of my dad's relationships. She is four years younger than me. So, when I was twenty-two, and she was eighteen, I decided that I wanted to find her. My understanding is that a couple of years after my mom and dad divorced, my dad met Amanda's mom. They were together only for a short time, but during that time, they got pregnant with her. Their relationship essentially ended up being a repeat of the relationship between my mom and dad.

Through the assistance of local law enforcement and her school system, I found Amanda. I remember sitting in the principal's office at Amanda's school, just thirty minutes away from Huntsville in Athens, Alabama. The principal told me that she was at school that day, but that he couldn't let me see her without her grandparent's consent. Imagine how I felt when I had never met my sister, finally finding her, sitting in the *same* building she was in, and not being able to see or talk to her for the first time!

I eventually received a phone call from Amanda's grandmother, Shirley, and she agreed for all of us to meet. I learned that Amanda lived with her grandparents because she and her mother didn't get along. Her mother lived right next door to them, but Amanda didn't have much interaction with her. To my knowledge, no one else in my dad's family had ever met Amanda. I would be the first!

Shirley was so happy and excited that we were meeting for the first time. She mentioned that this was like an "Oprah" moment. The first time I drove to meet Amanda at her grandparent's house, it was a long and emotional drive. I cried almost the entire way! When I arrived at the front door, I was a nervous wreck! Amanda came into the room to meet me, she hugged me, and told me things would be okay. My initial impression was that she seemed to be quiet and reserved. Amanda had brown hair like mine. We were both interested in modeling and had horrible tempers. I informed Amanda that her late grandfather had designed her high school, and a plaque with his name on it was hanging near the entrance. They shared the same last name, but she wasn't aware that her grandfather had designed her school. Our last name would end up being one of the few things that we had in common!

As time went on, I learned that Amanda had been arrested numerous times by the time she was in her late teens! She was abusing drugs and alcohol and led a terrible life. It was certainly not the reunion that I had hoped it would be! I saw her only a couple more times after I learned all of this about her. One of these times was when she had been in a serious car accident. I took off from work and drove the 100 miles to Birmingham to visit her in the hospital. Another time, I took her with me to my Aunt Donna's house in Mississippi at Christmastime. Donna is my dad's sister, and he was visiting Donna with four of our half-brothers. Although I had already met all of them through Mawmaw over the years, this was the first time that Amanda had ever met them.

I have another half-brother, Jessie, who I wouldn't meet until years later. Jessie was born out of a relationship that my dad had after my dad's relationship with Amanda's mom was over. To avoid any confusion, my mother only had two children. My dad has eight, as far as we know, by five different women. The breakdown is me with my mom, Amanda, with her mom, Jessie, with his mom, Jackie, Jonathan, Jamie, and Jasper, with their mom, and Josh, with his current wife. That is a lot to keep up with, isn't it? The family dynamics and dysfunction associated with all of these "families" have created many hurt feelings and resentments among everyone involved, and my dad is the common denominator in this crazy dysfunction. The result of this dysfunction is that I was not raised with my siblings, and I didn't get to know them well. It is no different for my siblings and just added to the family dynamics and dysfunction.

Mawmaw arranged for me to meet Jessie for the first time. The experience of meeting Jessie for the first time was *way* different than the one I had with Amanda. Jessie was in a relationship and had two small children at this time. He was quiet, reserved, and so kind to me. I could tell that he was a gentleman and genuinely happy to meet me. I believe Mawmaw was able to get in touch with Jessie because our other half-brothers had somehow found him. We stay in touch and occasionally get together to see each other.

Even as a young adult, it is hard to describe the level of confusion that was created by finally meeting and connecting with my siblings on my dad's side. I was trying to make sense of the dysfunction after hearing about how they grew up and their relationships with our dad. Almost every one of their mothers experienced physical abuse at the hands of our father. There were accusations of him being nearly non-existent and not providing for their emotional, physical, and financial needs. Only the four boys that had the same mother, Trish, were raised together, but they divorced when the boys were still young. Over the years, I would occasionally see Trish and the boys at Mawmaw's house. Trish was always very good to me. Again, the best way I can describe all of this to you is complete and utter family dysfunction.

For a while, after ending my relationship with Kyle, I was happy with my independence and freedom. I didn't make a lot of money, but I had a brand-new apartment, a nice car, paid all my bills, and kept to myself. I withdrew and became a very private person. I didn't know what I wanted to do as far as a career, but I knew I didn't like having many rules, nor was I willing to give up my new found freedom. I would occasionally go to church, and when I didn't go, I felt guilty and shameful. I would think about the church I attended in Collierville, the things that I experienced, the love and support of the people, and the many seeds that were planted during those years.

I recall that many of my interactions with Mom seemed more like a competition between sisters than mother and daughter. I would call her names, talk ugly to her, and make references to how I was going to make more out of myself and have more in life than her. I would even say hurtful things like she didn't deserve to have children. She would get defensive and tell me that I wouldn't do any better at raising kids, to which I would say that I wasn't going to have kids, to prove a point. On more than one occasion, when I was arguing with my mom, I asked her why she even had children, to which her response was, "I could have done something about it!" I understand that she was being defensive, but it was still a defining moment for me. This unresolved conflict with my mother would continue to be one of the few constants in my life.

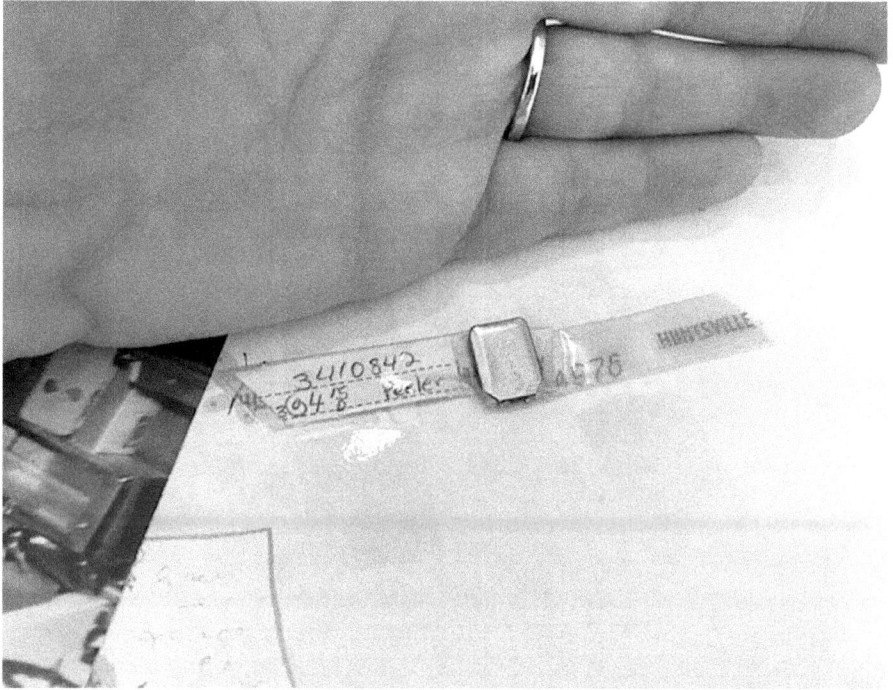

Hospital bracelet from my birth

DAILY WEIGHT LIST	DATE	WT.
1-88	10/27	3-8
1460	10/30	3-3½
1460	10/31	3-8½
1432	11/1	3-8½
1375	11/2	3-7½
1418	11/3	3-3
1418	11/4	3-7
1403	11/5	3-1½
	11/6	3-2½
	11-7	3-3
	11-8	3-5
	11-9	3-5½
	11-10	3-5
	11-11	3-7½
	11-12	3-8½
	11-13	3-10
	11-14	3-11½
	11-15	3-12
	11-16	3-13
	11-17	3-14½
	11-18	4-15
	11-19	4-1
	11-20	4-3
	11-21	4-3
	11-22	
	11-23	4-6½
	11-24	4-9
	11-25	4-10¼
	11-26	4-11½
	1-27	4-12½
	11-28	4-14
	11-29	5-1
	11-30	5-1½
	12-1	5-3½
	12-2	5-6
	12-3	5-8
	12-4	

Hospital weight chart from my time in the NICU

Lying on a hand-made crocheted afghan that
Mawmaw made for me when I was an infant

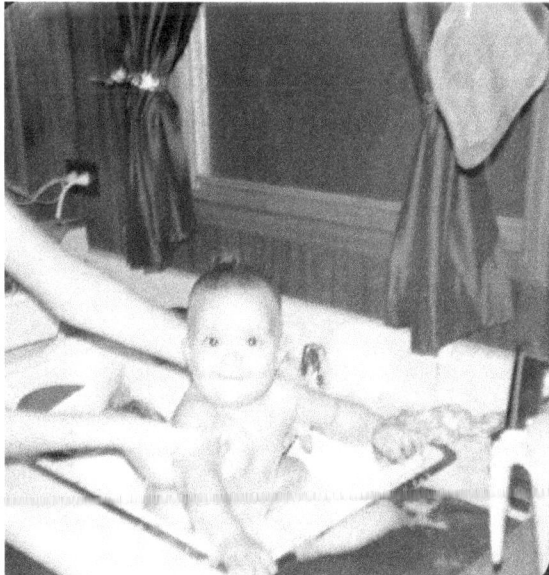

Mom and Dianne are bathing me in
the kitchen sink at Dianne's house

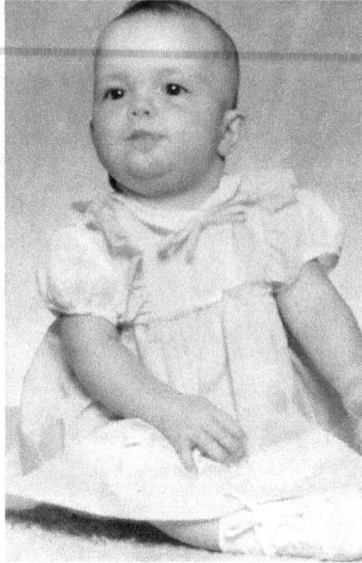

Granddaddy told me that I was "showing off" for the camera in this picture

Playing outside at Grandmama and Granddaddy's house

Riding a green tricycle in the driveway at Grandmama and Granddaddy's house

My favorite Easter picture of me growing up, at three-years-old, wearing my beautiful dress that had bells sewn into the underside of the skirt

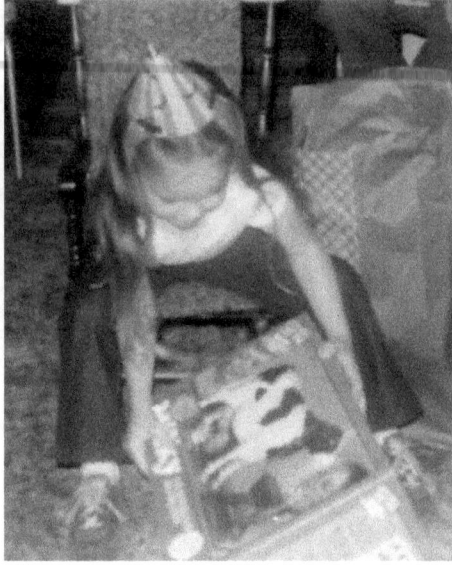

Celebrating my 4th birthday party at Nanny's house wearing my Halloween party hat

One of my favorite modeling photos from a photoshoot in 2006

Me at 38 years old

Our favorite wedding photo

Another photo from our beautiful wedding in June 2015

Ready for a date night in 2017

Attending a local charity ball in 2018

Our favorite photo from our fifth wedding anniversary photoshoot

Chapter 7

Happily Never After

My mom was divorced for several years before meeting her current husband, Greg, at her job. Before she did, she had become super independent, having spent many years dating on-again and off-again. I had become super independent, as well. I was so happy for my mom that she had found love and someone that would be a good father-figure to Shaun.

Greg and I were talking one time, and he shared with me that Mom had told him a few stories about me growing up. Greg was in absolute shock when Mom mentioned that I loved to watch TV wrestling with Granddaddy. Greg said that it completely changed his perception and image that had of me growing up! I can't help but laugh about this because I did go through that short-lived tomboy phase, but I am such a girly-girl now.

One day, I was enjoying some time off in my apartment. I had decided to order some food at a local delivery place called Steak-Out. The driver that delivered the food to my door was attractive and super kind! He was so helpful that I decided to call the restaurant manager and provide positive feedback. I know that most of the time, managers receive complaints, and I wanted to report something good about his delivery service. I don't recall the exact words of my compliment concerning Chris, but apparently, it was good enough that Chris called me and asked me out on a date!

Chris lived nearby me at the time, and after about a month of dating, we moved in together. We each had small one-bedroom apartments, so we moved into a larger two-bedroom apartment. Looking back after all these years, it's interesting how I can recall specific events in childhood, but I can't remember much about this entire relationship. It is almost as if I have blocked most of it out of my mind.

A couple of months after we moved in together, we were engaged. I didn't like Chris' mother, and she certainly didn't care for me. It placed a considerable strain on our relationship. I didn't even want her at our wedding. To me, if she disliked me so much, then she didn't deserve to come to *my* wedding. We decided to get married in Tennessee. We didn't invite anyone because I didn't want any issues.

After the newness of our relationship wore off, our fighting began to escalate. The family issues with his mother didn't help matters. Chris got laid off due to new driver rules and regulations at his delivery job, and my family was kind enough to provide him with temporary employment at their business. While this helped, we still had financial issues. Finances were only one of the marital problems contributing to our failing marriage. We were both still getting used to married life.

I was only twenty-three when Chris and I met. My closest girlfriends were single, and I kept hanging out with them, while Chris' closest friend was single, and he kept hanging out with him. Chris and I would make criticizing remarks toward each other and about each other's families. We were both defensive and blamed each other for the way that we were behaving. Ultimately, we weren't ready to face the typical struggles of married life, nor did we have enough in common. We divorced a short time later. Chris and I should have never gotten married. It's not that I didn't care for Chris, but we certainly didn't take enough time to get to know each other and had we done so, I don't believe we would have married.

It was during my relationship with Chris in 1997 that I first noticed my anxiety and had my first actual panic attack. I was driving on the interstate in Huntsville and began to feel dizzy and light-headed. The panic came from out of nowhere! It scared me so much that I pulled over at a nearby store and had the store clerk call for an ambulance! I had no idea what was happening to me! After being evaluated at the hospital, the doctors diagnosed me with anxiety and informed me that I had experienced a panic attack.

Following my divorce from Chris, I met a couple of different men and lived with each of them, back to back. In hindsight, I believe that I was trying to correct my mistake of divorce. I found out that you can't fix a mistake by making more! I couldn't stand the word "divorce." It's like a mark that is stamped on you forever. The stigma of shame surrounding divorce feels like it permeates you, especially until you can say that you are "married" again. Even then, it doesn't completely go away. I don't like that there is a box on any form that you have to check if you are "divorced" or how it seems that society, in general, judges you for being divorced. Over the years, I have felt judged by people for having been divorced. I have found that it is especially true when they have never experienced one, and sadly, it has usually been within the church. It is hurtful, and I think it is awful when this happens. I heard a pastor explain it this way once during a sermon on marriage and divorce within the church, "Just because you have never been divorced, it doesn't mean that you're in a Godly marriage."

It was around this time in my life that I was visiting my best friend, Tammy, who had moved to Nashville, Tennessee. The following story is not easy to discuss, but I feel it is necessary due to the level of impact it had on my life. I have Tammy's permission to share this story, and out of respect for her and our long-standing friendship, I will not share any details leading up to the event. However, those particular details are not relevant to the point that I am attempting to convey to you.

I will begin by saying that Tammy and I made a horrible decision that got us both arrested! The worst part was that we didn't even *have* to be. We *chose* to be hard-headed and were mouthing off at each other to the point that the police had no choice but to arrest us. The police officers were even kind enough to hint around and let us know all this was not necessary. Friends, this is what stubborn looks like right here, and where it will take you. Tammy and I were both in our mid-twenties when we got arrested in Nashville, and it would be a defining moment in my life.

I can assure you that you don't ever want to go to jail! Whatever you have heard, it is likely to be everything they said it is and more. It didn't help that this was in Nashville, TN, and not in a smaller or more rural location. At first, Tammy and I were still together when we initially arrived at intake. Neither of us had ever been to jail before, and neither of us has been to jail since. We were mortified when the correctional officers walked us past the men's section! We thought they were going to place us in the holding cell with them. It was likely naïve thinking, but we just didn't understand why they took us that route. The correctional officer laughed and said, "We are not going to stick you in there with them." That was a relief, but then it happened, they separated us! I can tell you that the incident that led up to us going to jail was not worth being separated from my best friend and not knowing what was going to happen next. What happened next was that I got lost in the system, but I didn't know it yet.

These twelve hours of agony would consist of me having to strip down naked in front of correctional officers to be searched. I had to take a shower in front of strangers using an itty-bitty container about the size of a ketchup holder from a fast food restaurant of what was supposed to be all-in-one soap and shampoo to bathe your whole body. I'm not sure why I was surprised. It was jail, not a country club! I got one phone call, so I called my mom. We argued more about what I had done to get in jail than how I was going to get out. When you are in jail, your only objective is to get out! Next, I had to get medical shots. I despise needles, so getting shots in jail took this experience to another level.

At first, I was in a jail cell with just me and one other girl. Is it sad that I remember that her name was Angel? Well, Angel wasn't an "angel" but was a prostitute and a "regular" in the jail. While Angel left me alone and slept most of the time, I was on the floor in an absolute panic. I was on the cold hard floor in my cell, continually alternating between praying and talking myself down from having a panic attack. I could not stop praying. *All* I had was God, as I was sitting there on the cold floor, terrified and panicked! I couldn't escape. I didn't know who was coming to get me or when I would be able to leave. If you want to spin up a control freak into a whirlwind, just put them in a cell and lock the door! Did I mention that I was claustrophobic, and I don't like tight spaces?

After what seemed like an eternity, the correctional officers moved me to a larger cell with several women. I use the term "women" loosely. These were not "ladies," as far as their demeanor. I was still scared to death. At least in the other cell, Angel left me alone. One girl commented on how she liked my Nike Air Max shoes. I was thinking, "Does she want to steal them?" Another girl kept messing with my naturally curly hair. I remember thinking that if I told her to stop, that I would probably get into a fight with her, so I just let her continue. I was relieved when she eventually stopped. Listening to the women talk in the cell, I discovered that most of these ladies were prostitutes and "regulars," just like Angel. Of course, Angel was on a first-name basis with most of these girls in this large cell with me!

All I could think about was being ashamed. While the female jailer was walking me from the small cell to the larger cell, she asked me why I was so quiet. I said, "I don't have anything to say." I was thinking, "What in the world do you want me to say?" Was I supposed to ask, "Hey, are you having a good day at work?" My mind was on my one mission: TO GET OUT!

I repeatedly asked myself, "Why did I get myself into this, and how am I going to get myself out?" I promised myself that when I got out of jail, I would never do anything to go back. A few of the ladies decided they were going to do some sort of drugs that they had snuck into the jail. I was utterly horrified. I had no idea what they had, and I didn't even look in their direction. I just heard them talking about getting high. I made sure that I was by the door in the front of the cell, and as far away as I could be from the ladies using their drugs in the back of the cell. I tried to act as if I was tired, which I was, so they would hopefully leave me alone. I did this by nonchalantly laying my head in my hand, covering part of my nose, and pretending to be asleep. No one noticed what I was doing. I tried to stay away from everyone, and for the most part, people left me alone.

Eventually, I was bailed out by an ex-boyfriend, which is a whole other story. Did I mention I was desperate to get out of jail? I say "eventually" because when he arrived at the jail, there were issues with my paperwork, and they had lost me in the system. The correctional officers in charge of out-processing had to figure out where I was inside the jail. He waited a few hours for them to find me and process me for release on bail. Tammy and I went to court, and the prosecutors dropped the charge on both of us. It was a minor charge, and we had never been in trouble before this incident. Thank you, Lord!

Tammy and I resumed our friendship a few months later when we accidentally ran into each other in an elevator. I don't believe this was a coincidence. I believe it was a God moment! Tammy and I have been friends for over thirty-five years, and she is my closest friend. She has been my friend longer than anyone else, and we haven't had a single issue since! I will reiterate that you do not ever want to go to jail! However, to soften the blow, do Tammy and I joke amongst each other from time to time about, "Remember way back when we went to jail?" We don't talk about it very often, but we can now laugh about our very own "Thelma and Louise" moment.

Most of you are probably wondering why I would choose to tell this embarrassing story voluntarily. The reason is that this event is a perfect example of a life-changing concept that I learned about during my recovery journey. The point is that we must look back on the things that we can't change and learn from those experiences. View them from a learning perspective and not a judgmental one. We must accept our past and the consequences of our actions, but realize that those experiences made us who we are today. Be grateful that whatever you have learned from your past has made you a better you!

This event reminds me of a woman that spoke at a seminar I attended over twenty years ago. She was telling us about her life journey. She was a middle-aged woman and had three sons: a criminal, a cop, and a lawyer. She said, "I have a son that likes to commit crimes, one that will arrest him for those crimes, and an attorney to bail him out!" I recall this story, even though it was over twenty years ago because that woman was able to take some painful aspects of her life and find some humor in them. It took vulnerability on her part to share her journey, and I am thankful she did because she taught me to find the silver lining and humor in even the most painful parts of our lives. If part of my journey helps you to do that, then I've accomplished my purpose.

Around this time, my Aunt Denise and Uncle Monte had another son, Taylor. Taylor was named after my Granddaddy, and it is one of my favorite names. Taylor is my Granddaddy's surname. Unfortunately, I didn't have the opportunity to spend much time with Taylor while he was growing up because I was already an adult, and they lived out of state. Monte is a mechanic and owns a repair shop. Taylor shares this love of vehicles, and they still enjoy restoring vehicles together in their spare time.

Around the time I turned 25, I decided that I wanted to attend modeling and acting school. I worked hard to save enough money to cover my tuition and to graduate from the program. Most people think that modeling is only about photoshoots or fashion shows, but this is only partially true. Modeling involves learning so much more than how to participate in these events. Modeling school has application to our daily lives, as well. For example, the classes covered poise, posture, hair, cosmetics, manners, etiquette, speaking, and sophistication. I loved learning all of these things. It taught me confidence, to a certain degree, at least on the outside.

There were many times that I was confident on the outside, but I felt like an emotional train wreck on the inside. During these "train wreck" moments, I would sometimes share how I felt with my mother. She would brush off my feelings in disbelief that I would feel this way about myself, instead of genuinely listening and trying to understand why I would feel that way. There were many times in my life that I did not feel that I could talk to my mother without feeling bad, shamed, or misunderstood. I believe that this is one of the reasons why we have not gotten along for most of my life.

As far as modeling, I participated in fashion runway shows at colleges and malls, for charity events, and was a promotional spokesperson for products such as Fossil, Dove, and Pantene. While these jobs were fun and exciting, I didn't start out doing them. There were many not-so-great jobs at first, to include one that involved me spinning a silly prize wheel at an RV convention. The things we will do to gain visibility and experience!

One of the things I liked most about modeling was the attention I received from people that didn't know me. No one knew or cared about my mistakes or what I had done in the past. They only knew that I was good at modeling. I was just an attractive stranger playing a *role*. I could be whatever I needed or wanted to be in the environment I was placed in for the job. Most of the time, I didn't have to speak, which made playing the role that much easier. All I had to do was *look* the part. At this point in my life, I was still somewhat reserved and had not fully come out of my shell. Unfortunately, I was exposed to the ugly side of modeling, as well. Let's just say that I would occasionally receive offers to do things that were in bad taste, and that would shame myself and my family. When this would happen, I would refuse the offer and walk away from the meeting or situation.

When I was twenty-six years old, I met Jason. He was a friend of the family and worked at the same company that Mom and Greg worked for at the time. The first time we met was at my mom's house. Unbeknownst to me at the time, my relationship with Jason would almost be a repeat of the one I had with Chris. Our relationship was intense in the beginning, and we became engaged after six months. Early on, his mother and I had some issues, but our relationship improved over time. We were married after being together for one year. We held the ceremony inside a small chapel located at a beautiful wedding venue on the top of a mountain in Huntsville, with about fifty guests in attendance.

Our marriage only lasted four and a half years and was filled with constant change and stress. We moved out of state to Texas after only having been married nine months and to Pennsylvania a year later. We moved so that Jason could further his career, and I was extremely homesick. Until I was married to Jason, I had not wanted to have children. I became open to it for a while during our marriage, but that changed once I began to question whether our marriage would last.

There were several reasons why I struggled with the issue of having children. For the most part, I never wanted children because of the way that I came into the world, parenting looked overwhelmingly difficult, and I didn't want the lifelong responsibility. I certainly didn't want to have a child with the wrong person or bring a child up in the dysfunction that I experienced growing up between both sides of my family.

Growing up, I felt as if I didn't have the freedom or the means to do what I wanted to do when I wanted to do it. Therefore, I decided early in my life that if I ever did achieve the means or freedom, I wouldn't give it up for anything. I am not saying that I don't love children or babies, because I do, but not enough to have any of my own and to have that lifelong commitment.

I vowed to myself that I would never be a single-mom like my mother. I grew up watching her struggle trying to raise and provide for Shaun and me. I knew that I didn't want that life for myself or my child.

Jason and I attended church for most of the year that we lived in the Dallas-Fort Worth area. I still had severe issues with driving, especially on the interstate. I didn't help that "everything is bigger in Texas," as they say! The interstates and ramps were very intimidating to me! Sometimes, I get anxious about my anxiety! What I mean by this is that my *fear* of having a panic attack can actually bring on a panic attack. I grew up in the city, but Huntsville is nothing like Dallas-Fort Worth! Since I had severe issues with driving, we had to take back roads to get everywhere. I tried a few different doctor-prescribed medications to relieve my anxiety, but I never found a medication that seemed to help without experiencing adverse side effects. There were times that my driving anxiety would be worse than other times. I don't know how to explain it, other than I *never* knew when I would experience a panic attack. It was usually more comfortable to take the back roads and not risk having a panic attack.

Jason and I stayed in Texas for a year, only to move to Pennsylvania for his job. The move would ultimately lead to the demise of our relationship. We lived in rural Pennsylvania for two years. The small town where we lived is one of the oldest cities in the United States. The way of life and how people lived was so different from the way I was used to living in Alabama. It was evident that we were not from the area, and most of the locals did not treat us well. I was not happy in Pennsylvania. There was nothing that I liked about the community, and I was so far away from Alabama.

Jason and I began arguing and fighting about anything and everything. I gained weight and was the largest I have even been in my life. My average weight is between 125-135lbs, and after one year in Pennsylvania, I weighed 165lbs. I had become very depressed, and I'm sure Jason was, too. I met with my family doctor, and he prescribed me an anti-depressant. The medication helped me to an extent, but for me, it did not address the *root cause* of my unhappiness.

We decided to try a marital separation, and I temporarily moved back to Alabama. Eventually, I moved back to Pennsylvania because I wanted to work things out. Our marriage quickly returned to the way they were before we separated. I found a job when I moved back to Pennsylvania and started making friends at work. Most of them were single and liked to party. They were not a good influence on me, and I began hanging out with them outside of work. We would usually go to the local bar, and I started drinking heavily. There were weekends where I didn't want to go home, and I would stay with one of my friends from work.

This small town in Pennsylvania was a very depressing area to live in, and there wasn't much to do. It wasn't unusual to see snow on the ground eight months out of the year. The weather was so nasty and cold, as compared to northern Alabama. When you add up everything: small town in a rural area, unfriendly locals, nothing to do, the weather, and no family nearby, it was overwhelming. I was self-medicating, and my problems only worsened with alcohol. I was disappointed with myself, and I knew that I was self-destructing.

Our marriage was hanging on by a thread. Jason knew this, and I was able to convince him to find a job in Alabama. He was able to find one forty-five minutes from Huntsville. I was so happy to move back to Alabama. However, Jason had a great job and loved the company he was working for in Texas and Pennsylvania. He left the company when he moved us back to make *me* happy. I had wholeheartedly believed that if we had the support from our family and friends again, it would help our marriage. I was mistaken, as this would only help *me*. Jason did not feel the same way, hence why this was one of our points of contention. He didn't require that he live near his family, because his focus was on climbing the corporate ladder and doing whatever was required of him to get to the top.

After we moved back to Alabama, things were okay for a while. However, Jason was resentful for having left the job that he loved, and I felt that our marriage had sustained too much damage from everything that happened in Texas and Pennsylvania. We got a divorce nine months after we moved back to Alabama. In hindsight, I question whether Jason and I should have just stayed friends and never gotten married. Jason was, and still is, a good man. I was drawn to the hope of stability and was trying to cover up the failure of my first divorce.

Jason was rehired by his former employer following our divorce and moved out of Alabama. The ironic thing about my broken relationship with Jason is that we still kept in touch. After a couple of years, we began to talk more often, but strictly as great friends. When he would come back to Alabama to visit his family, we would usually get together. We would go out to eat, shop, and have great conversations. At one point, we almost reconciled, but quickly realized that it would have been a mistake. Again, Jason is a good person, but ultimately, we just didn't have much in common.

Following my divorce, I was fortunate to be hired for a position at a government defense contractor in Huntsville. Although it wasn't what I would have initially chosen for a career, being in an active role supporting our military was a unique and special calling. I worked at this company for almost a decade, held several different positions of varying responsibilities, and earned five promotions. Since I was single, this job provided me the financial stability and excellent benefits I desired. I took a few college courses but eventually stopped because I realized that I wouldn't earn any more money than I was currently making on my job. I have always been good at sales and possess a strong entrepreneurial spirit. The downside is there isn't much security and stability in that type of career, especially for a single person.

While working at this job, I met my good friend, Wayne. I like to call Wayne my "second" dad. We have had so many conversations about faith, fun, and relationships. It didn't matter if we were having a good laugh or a serious discussion; I loved being around and talking with Wayne. We are both feisty, and we could hold an intense debate, but they were all in love!

I went through a short phase of going to local bars with my girlfriends after finalizing my divorce from Jason. During this phase, a mutual friend introduced me to my friend, Charles. He is a great friend and is like a brother to me to this day! I would be single for the next ten years and would have three serious relationships during that time. Each one of these relationships lasted exactly nine months. I am not quite sure what was significant about the nine-month timeframe, but that is how long they lasted. I enjoyed my independence, but I did want to find someone to share my life with someday. I never dated for the sake of dating, because I am the type of girl that is looking for a committed relationship.

One of these nine-month relationships was with Patrick. After we dated for a few months, Patrick moved into my apartment. Patrick and I thought that we would eventually get married, so we decided to get a house together. Grandmama was getting older, and her health started to deteriorate. Grandmama passed away on the same day and just hours before our scheduled home closing. She died from Pulmonary Hypertension. I went to see my Grandmama one last time, who had just passed away in her living room, before rushing off to my home closing appointment. I was overwhelmed and devastated. I also became angry, and rage took over.

I began to grieve. I didn't know how to grieve. I never had to grieve anyone in my life. Grandmama was like a second mother to me for many years. She would lie down with me at night in her spare bedroom and tell me to close my eyes and count to ten. I was afraid of the dark, so she said to me that after I counted down and opened my eyes, the room would be much lighter. Grandmama was right. It worked! Grandmama was part of the glue that held my family together. She was always there for me. She loved to watch Charles Stanley on television. I think she did this since she and Granddaddy didn't go to church for many years. However, during the last few years leading up to her passing, they began to go to church regularly together.

After she died, I constantly had dreams about her. My world around me was falling apart, and I had no idea how to deal with these feelings. I remember worrying about what I would do if I ever lost her and my Granddaddy one day. As a child, I even recall worrying about this! Patrick couldn't do anything right in my eyes, and he didn't understand my grief. He would leave food out overnight on the counter after he had come home from work, and I would just go into a full-blown rage. While doing our laundry, he dumped the detergent powder onto our clothes, instead of letting the powder dissolve in the water before adding our clothes. I went into a full-blown blackout rage. He didn't know how to be there for me. I didn't know how to help myself. In my eyes, nothing would help bring Grandmama back!

There were other issues, besides my rage, in our relationship. Within the first couple of weeks of moving into our house, Patrick's attitude seemed to change. It either changed toward me, or it was there all along under the surface, and I didn't see it until we purchased the house. He worked second shift and started going to strip clubs and bars with his friends, instead of coming home. To make matters worse, he would turn his cell phone off while he was out with his friends. It was the proverbial straw that broke the camel's back. His behavior was a trigger for me due to experiencing similar behavior in some of my previous relationships. I was also hurt because I felt that I supported him emotionally and allowed him to move in with me while he was attending the police academy, but he couldn't support me with the loss of Grandmama.

When I confronted him about his behavior, he told me that he was not willing to change, which was a non-negotiable for me. I ended our relationship. Fortunately for me, before signing on our home, I made Patrick pay the remaining four payments of my apartment lease. I moved back into my apartment, and we were able to sell the house within one week of ending our relationship. I always had trust issues, especially when it came to men. I had been hurt too many times. I always had a backup plan to protect myself…always!

The week after my relationship ended with Patrick, I was out on the town with one of my girlfriends and met Bryant. Bryant was the most handsome man, and he was a gentleman to me. He seemed to be the one to "save the day," and it helped me take the focus off of my grieving. Bryant was a Christian and came from a religious family. He lived out of state and worked as a police officer, but was temporarily in Huntsville for six weeks attending a training course. I happened to meet him at the beginning of his training. We fell in love quickly and spent every evening and all of the weekends together. We were both in our mid-30s, and Bryant's parents called and talked to him every single day. I remember thinking how strange it was to me for Bryant to be in his mid-30s and having to speak to his parents every day. At most, I talked to my family for a few minutes every couple of weeks. It felt like they were continually interrupting what little time we had to spend together.

At the end of Bryant's six-week training, he was packing up and getting ready to go back home to New Mexico. We were both broken-hearted and devastated. About midway home on his drive home, Bryant called me. His voice was shaky, and he was very nervous. He said, "I know this may sound crazy, and I don't know all the details of how this will work, but I just want you to think about this. I want you to think about marrying me." A few weeks later, Bryant came to visit me, and he officially proposed to me. Since he had a lot of frequent flyer miles saved up, and his work schedule was four days on, and four days off, he determined that he could visit me every three weeks. He did precisely this for the next year.

After I chose a beautiful white wedding dress for the ceremony, my mother told my aunts that she couldn't believe that I was wearing a white wedding dress because "it's her *third* marriage, after all." Her saying this hurt me deeply. I had a minor surgery scheduled, and Bryant flew in to be with me. I asked mom to be there for my surgery, as well. She didn't know that Bryant was going to be there. She got mad that I asked her to come up and she left as soon as she knew Bryant was there with me. I was so upset. The point wasn't that he was there and she didn't *need* to be there. I wanted her, *in addition to* Bryant, to be there with me for support. She missed this entire point, and this was yet another time that she wasn't there for me.

The year that Bryant was visiting me was an emotional rollercoaster for both of us. In the times leading up to our visits, it was just pure joy and excitement. However, saying goodbye was awful. Frequently, he would be jealous of the time I spent with friends when he was home in New Mexico and couldn't be there with me. We had to rely strictly on the phone to communicate and stay in touch. It was easier for Bryant to come to visit me because I was afraid to fly, and he had frequent flyer miles. He had four days off at a time, and I only had the weekends off.

Tensions would sometimes get high on the phone. There were so many details to iron out before we could get married. We had to figure out where we were going to live. Bryant had to find employment. He also had a lot of debt to pay off. I explained to him that the only way we would even have a chance of making it work was for him to pay off some of his debt, which he started to do. Bryant had credit card debt and several vehicles, including ATV's and a motorcycle. I needed to feel financially secure and didn't see how we would have much of a chance of staying together if we started our marriage in debt. Things became so stressful at times, and Bryant would just shut down.

It was during these stressful times that Bryant would get so upset and frustrated with me, that he would break-up with me on the phone. He wouldn't talk to me! There would be no working on things during this time. He wouldn't even explain his thoughts to me and everything that he was feeling. He forced me to sit and wait for days or weeks before he would respond. It was devastating to me. He did this to me at least twice during our engagement. Despite this, I was desperate to hang on to this relationship with him. I was so in love with him, and I convinced myself that it was the distance that was tearing us apart. We chose to get married on Valentine's Day of 2009.

In the days leading to the wedding, I had been forthright with him and expressed all of my fears. Bryant decided that he would move to Alabama, get a lateral transfer on his job, and hope to get into the police academy. He moved to Huntsville a few weeks before our wedding day. I had significant concerns in the days leading up to the wedding, but I thought it was just me having cold feet.

The day of the wedding came, and we held the ceremony. It was a small ceremony that was held at the same wedding venue that Jason and I had been married, except it was held outside and not inside the chapel. I know what you are thinking. I don't understand why in the world I chose the same place, other than the fact that it is one of the most beautiful venues in Huntsville. During the ceremony, I was nauseous. I don't recall smiling, and I certainly wasn't feeling as if this was the best day of my life. I remember Bryant's father hugging me and whispering in my ear, "Take care of my son." The way he said it to me gave me an eerie feeling.

Following the ceremony, we started to drive to our honeymoon in Tennessee. Less than an hour into the drive, I freaked out! I asked Bryant to pull his truck over because I was physically ill to my stomach. As much as I thought I loved this man, I felt that I had made a colossal mistake! It wasn't cold feet that I was experiencing; it was pure fear. Fear that this man would not let us live without his family interfering daily, fear that he wouldn't get on with the local police department, and fear that he wouldn't get out of debt. The thing I feared most of all was that when the going got tough, he would shut down just as he had previously done multiple times in our relationship. I was afraid that he would leave or give up on us. He agreed that we had made a mistake.

We immediately called the chapel. The officiate assured us that we needed to turn the truck around and return to the chapel. When we arrived at the chapel, the officiate explained to us that of all the marriages he had performed, he had never had this happen. He said, "I only performed a ceremony. Turning in the license to the courthouse and the Probate Office processing it, is what officially marries you. I can simply rip up the license, never turn it into the courthouse, and a legal marriage never took place. I can do this if you both agree to it right now." We were relieved to hear that this could be done and decided it was the best course of action.

Did we just humiliate ourselves in front of our entire family and waste a lot of money and time? Yes. Would it be embarrassing to explain everything to everyone that was involved or knew that he had supposedly gotten married? Yes. Ultimately, I believe God was watching out for both of us. It would be one of the most painful lessons of my life. People talked about me behind my back, and I was called a "Runaway Bride" and a few other things that I should not repeat. Bryant moved back to New Mexico and found a place on the *same* street as his parents. He eventually married a woman that was just as family-oriented as he is, and they now have four children.

It took me five years to fully heal from my relationship with Bryant. I never intended to hurt anyone, especially Bryant. I knew in my heart that God had forgiven me, but knowing the pain that I had caused myself and others ate away at my core. I knew that all of this was between God and me, and no one else's responsibility. As I healed, I continuously asked God to lead me to the correct man and promised Him that when he did, that I'd be sure this would never happen again.

Chapter 8

Terrible Loss and Wonderful Gain

Not long after Grandmama passed away, I was shocked and upset to learn that Granddaddy had a girlfriend. The day I met her, I thought it was a lady from their church that was coming over to visit. I was wrong. I didn't much care for her. I knew Grandmama was gone, and she wasn't coming back. My family found out that this woman was someone Granddaddy previously knew from years ago. I had heard rumors of infidelity about Granddaddy over the years, as well as some other things. I'm not sure if I just wanted to put those things out of my mind, or if I couldn't wrap my head around them. Maybe, I didn't want to believe that a man that was such a great Granddaddy to me could do the things that some say he did.

In 2010, after having gone through the terrible break-up with Bryant, and being confused, I decided that I needed to get "saved" again. I felt this way for a few reasons: I didn't feel like I was "good enough" to get saved the first time. All of the years leading to this point, I repeatedly asked God to forgive me and felt so ashamed that I thought I had to ask God to save me over and over again. My church taught me, "once saved, always saved." Despite this, I felt I had sinned to the point of needing to be saved and baptized again. I suppose I wanted to be confident in my salvation, and I don't believe that I fully understood the meaning and the commitment the first time I got saved and baptized in the church at the age of fifteen.

I told my mom and invited her to come to my baptism. I wasn't surprised that she didn't show up, but it did hurt. While my mom didn't attend my baptism, Granddaddy and his girlfriend did show up. I could have cared less that his girlfriend was there, but Granddaddy being there was everything to me. I got baptized on the banks of the Tennessee River in south Huntsville. While everyone else stood, the church ensured that Granddaddy had a chair, so he could sit down and still have a good view of my baptism. Granddaddy being there and supporting me made all the difference in the world to me. It would be one of the most special moments I ever shared with him.

In August of 2010, my Granddaddy's health worsened, and everyone knew that his passing was imminent. He had a lot of fluid built up and was in the hospital. When I visited him, he told me, "Tammy, don't eat bad your whole life!" He told me this because he knew that he had eaten unhealthy his entire life, and it was a major contributing factor in his death from Congestive Heart Failure.

In the weeks leading up to his passing, he was under the care of hospice in his living room. It was the same spot in the living room that Grandmama had been when hospice came in to care for her. During these weeks, Granddaddy still had his sense of humor about him. While sitting in the living room with him one day, I said, "Granddaddy, you have lived a lot of years, do you have any words of wisdom?" He said, "Yes, just because you see a brown cow, doesn't mean you are going to get chocolate milk!" I laughed so hard! I don't know why I would have expected any other answer than a humorous one. Another one of my favorite sayings that Granddaddy once told me was, "If you don't want someone to get your goat, then don't tell them where it's tied!" Granddaddy had so many of these sayings.

Granddaddy was a very passive man, and almost everything was a joke. He was also extremely tender-hearted, though he didn't want you to see that side of him. I do recall him falling apart in the hallway of the hospital when Grandmama had a triple bypass a few years prior. I know on my wedding day to Jason, he was a mess with tears because he was emotional about me getting married. Mom told me that he was so upset when we were moving away years ago with Alan to Louisiana that Granddaddy put his sunglasses on so we couldn't see his eyes filling with tears. I could count on one hand the number of times I had seen him cry in my lifetime.

I was the last family member to see him before he took his last breath in his living room that day. He passed thirty minutes after I left the house. The last time I saw him was special to me, and I will always remember it. I had an extraordinary bond with Granddaddy, from my birth to the end of his life. That makes me feel so good to know he loved me so much. He was more than a father-figure to me; he was both a Granddaddy and a Daddy to me!

I gave a eulogy at Granddaddy's funeral. It was one of the hardest things I have ever done in my life. I told my favorite stories about Granddaddy. I described the Easter egg hunts, him teaching me to ride a bike and a few other stories. One of the best stories that I told was one he had told me a few years before his death. When I was a toddler, he had taken me to the local fair. One of the games at the fair was the Duck Pond Game. If you aren't familiar with this game, it's where numerous toy ducks are swimming around in a pond, and each duck has a number on the bottom. You choose one duck in the pond, and the number on the bottom determines the prize you receive. Well, I threw a fit, actually a duck fit, because I didn't want the prize that I won. I wanted to keep the *actual* duck. Granddaddy slipped the fair worker a dollar so that I could have the duck. I've always enjoyed feeding the ducks in a pond located in downtown Huntsville called Big Spring Park. When I got up to speak about Granddaddy at his funeral, I brought a large yellow rubber duck up to the podium with me. As I finished telling all of my favorite stories about Granddaddy, I said, "Since Granddaddy gave me a rubber duck many years ago, I'd like to give him one back." I then walked over and placed the eulogy notes that I had just read, along with the large rubber duck inside his casket. I wanted those memories to go with him, and I will always remember being able to share my favorite memories of Granddaddy at his funeral.

I woke up one morning in my apartment a few weeks after Granddaddy was gone, and I don't know how to explain it any other way than I thought that I was losing my mind! The feelings of grief and panic just hit me out of nowhere. I didn't know how I was going to go on in my life without him. I was experiencing those same feelings of grief again that I felt after Grandmama passed. I didn't know what to do with them or how to handle them! My anger got the best of me. I began raging again, and I took things out on others that I would deeply regret. I was feeling *constant* rage and anxiety. During this time, a neighbor friend of mine gave me a dog named Abby because she and her husband were moving into an assisted living home. I would have Abby for about a year. Abby served a meaningful purpose and provided me much comfort during this time in my life, but I felt horrible that I had to leave her at home for extended lengths of time while I was at work. Abby was used to having someone always at home, and now she was spending most of the time by herself. I eventually gave Abby to my cousin, Rebecca.

For a couple of years after Granddaddy had passed, I would go line-dancing every weekend. At the time, there was only one bar where you could go line-dancing in Huntsville. Most people thought it was strange that I wouldn't drink, but I was strictly going to dance. Dancing was therapeutic for me. I would go every weekend because it was fun, was great physical exercise, and for the most part, it got my mind off my grandfather. Line-dancing is a very structured way to dance, and there isn't a way to do it without having to concentrate on what you are doing. It temporarily kept my mind busy and off my pain.

I was still getting over my relationship with Bryant, backing out of a marriage, and now losing one of the most influential people in my life. I didn't know how to process my feelings. To make matters worse, more and more information about Granddaddy's past started coming out. I didn't fully understand how, at times, he was supposedly as bad of a husband as he was to Grandmama and how bad of a father he was to my mom and her siblings. Now, this wasn't always the case, as he did a lot of good in his life, but I did begin to see how others could feel the way that they did towards him. It was confusing because all I ever saw and knew was that to *me*, he was a great Granddaddy!

I would periodically have dreams about Granddaddy, but not more than I would continue to have about Grandmama. They would be so realistic and lifelike that it was difficult to believe they were only a dream. One time, I had a dream about Grandmama, and she was a younger version of herself. She placed both of her hands on my face. It felt as real in my dream as if someone put their hands on my face right now!

One night, I had one of the most vivid dreams I have ever had in my life, and it is one that I will never forget: I was outdoors with a bunch of strangers in the middle of a terrifying storm. There was debris flying all around us from an enormous tornado that had formed. I looked up into the dark sky and saw a large opening. In the opening was Jesus. Next to him was God, but I couldn't see Him. I knew it was God because Jesus was talking to someone up there with Him through the open frame in the sky. At the same time that Jesus was talking to whom I believe was God, Jesus was reaching one hand down towards me, as if to save me from the horrific storm. He was asking God if He should take me or let me stay! It was at this point that my dream ended. To my recollection, this is the only dream I have ever had about God.

After my relationship with Bryant ended, the next five years went like this: I would date, date, and date some more. I learned that I liked to weed people out early. I usually went on a date or two with someone and *found* a reason why I didn't want to go out with them again. I desired companionship, but I was fearful of repeating the mistakes that I had made in the past. I was scared of being alone, but I was also scared to be vulnerable. I had a hard time trying to guard my heart in the past. It resulted in me going down the wrong paths and having many dark days. One time, I was speaking to my mom on the phone, and she told me she had been praying for me for years to find the right person for me. I was shocked, in a good way, because I don't remember a time that she had ever told me that she was praying for me. It made me feel so good to know she was praying for me.

During this time of dating, I would spend a lot of time with my friends, especially Charles. Neither of us was in a relationship, and we could always count on each other to be there when we needed someone. He is like family to me. We have now been friends for sixteen years. I also spent more time with Tammy, my best friend going back to middle school.

There were times that I was so lonely and depressed that I felt as if I didn't want to live. I never had any thoughts of harming myself, but just the fact that I had these feelings, I knew it wasn't healthy. One year on Christmas day, I experienced one of the lowest points in my life. I had visited with family earlier in the holiday season, but I was alone on Christmas day. I went to see a movie, had Waffle House for lunch, and then went back to the theater to see another movie. I thought to myself, "Look at me and my pathetic life." I never wanted to feel that alone again.

Over the years, I would mostly use online dating sites to find my dates. I got frustrated and gave up online dating for a time. Eventually, I decided that I would try "one last time." Leading up until now, I was so disgusted at the types of prospects I was meeting. In my online dating profile description, I decided I was going to be *brutally* open and honest. Not that I wasn't before, but this time I wasn't going to sugarcoat any of my feelings, and I didn't care who it might upset! My profile was a mile long. It was a long list of what I wanted, but now it contained an even longer list of what I didn't want. At the top of my "wanted list" was that the man I was looking for must be a Christian. He must be a gentleman. He must be romantic and have a good heart. He must be strong, yet sensitive. I also stated, in so many words, "I like to weed people out early, so don't waste my time if you aren't serious about meeting your soul-mate!" I wasn't shy about any of my intentions! I also disclosed some pretty funny things in the description. They were comical but true to me. In the middle of my profile, I said, "If I see another man on this dating site with his shirt off and holding up a dead animal, such as a deer or a fish, I am going to scream!" Remember, it wasn't uncommon to see such things, especially on dating sites in Alabama!

Usually, I would have numerous men message me on the site and start with, "Hey, what's up, hottie?" That is *all* they would say in an attempt to initiate a conversation with me. I was thinking, "You mean to tell me that you are trying to sell yourself on why I should give you a shot, and this is the best you've got? Are you kidding me?" One day, I opened my inbox and saw a message. In so many words, this is what it said:

Dear Ms. Tammy,
I read every word. In some portions of your profile, I laughed my head off, and in other parts, I could tell you know what you are looking for in a man. I think we have a lot in common. I would be interested in getting to know you better if you would like to do the same.
Clint

Wow! What? Could this be someone who is sincere about getting to know me?

I messaged Clint back, and we eventually exchanged phone numbers. We texted daily for almost a week. Clint asked if he could set up a date with me, on Friday at 6 pm, and take me to Olive Garden. He asked if he could pick me up from my apartment. I agreed.

I allowed Clint to pick me up, not because we had been talking for a week, but because of the content of the information we discussed and that we had exchanged some verifiable information. We knew we lived only twelve minutes away from each other, I knew he was Active Duty in the Army and had three children (two that still lived at home), and we both knew where each other worked. In a part of our conversations leading up to our date, we discussed certain Christian and relationship books we had both read, including *"The 5 Love Languages"*, *"His Needs, Her Needs,"* and *"Love & Respect."* Clint referred to these as the relationship trifecta! I figured if Clint had read the "trifecta," more than likely, it was safe to assume that he wasn't a serial killer!

Friday night finally came! Up until this point, Clint and I had only seen photos of each other. I answered my door and immediately thought that he was so handsome. Okay, so I at least know at this point how attracted I am to this man! Now, off to Olive Garden, we go. There was a long wait time at the restaurant, so until our table was ready, we sat in the bar area and talked. Leading up to meeting Clint, I had prayed to God and asked him to send me a man that loved to talk, and boy did He sure deliver! Clint loves to talk! Clint talked so much about his career and every aspect of it. He was nervous, and I could tell. At one point, I had to ask him not to talk about work so much. I think he got the hint. While I may have been the "Queen" of dating over the past decade, Clint hadn't dated in many years! He disclosed this fact to me before we met.

So, our table was ready, and we went to be seated. After we were seated, the real interview and interrogation began! Remember, I liked to weed out men early! I grilled Clint so hard (in a kind way) and asked him every question under the sun, but he didn't seem to mind. I was asking him some tough questions, and he was taking it all in stride. I also knew he was telling me the truth because I didn't necessarily like some of the answers to his questions. However, I respected the fact that he was telling me the truth, nonetheless! I think we talked for a good two hours or more at Olive Garden.

We decided to go back to my place and talk further in private and watch TV. On the short drive home in his truck, I knew that I wanted to date him exclusively already, and this first date wasn't even halfway over yet! Later on, I found out that he felt the same! We got back to my apartment, spent a lot more time talking and getting to know each other. It was the most comfortable thing ever. It was as if we had known each other for a long time! Clint kissed me for the first time, and that was a memorable moment for both of us.

Clint eventually had to leave and went home. Before he did, he had asked me if I wanted to meet his family the next day. Now, we had already decided that we wanted to keep seeing each other exclusively before he asked me to meet his family, but I was still shocked when he first asked me. I felt that it might be a bit soon, but I trusted his judgment and agreed. Later, I had found out that he thought the sooner his family and I met, the better. His kids were older, and they understood that he wouldn't just bring anyone home to meet them. With both of us being forty-one, we decided that when you know someone is the one, you just know! We both knew what we were looking for in life!

I went over to Clint's house the next morning. He had three children from his first marriage. His youngest two children, Rebekah, and Aaron, were still living at home. His third child, Ryan, was serving in the military and had recently married. The two at home were old enough that they would soon be transitioning out of the house. Clint and I fell in love very quickly. Our relationship moved fast, so fast that we got engaged after dating only six weeks! I know we shocked a lot of people, to include his kids still at home. The kids had not only been through one divorce with Clint and their mother, but they endured yet another divorce with Clint and another woman. His second marriage had ended just two years before me.

Clint and I didn't handle things as well as we could have on our parts, nor did we feel we deserved some of the reaction and treatment we received from the younger two kids. Eventually, the situation led to his two kids moving out of the house. I learned early on that the main reason why Clint's second marriage failed was due to the blended-family situation. Clint and I were certainly not going to let that happen in our relationship! We just didn't handle everything as well as we could have in the beginning, but neither did his youngest two children or their biological mom.

Clint and I were married in June of 2015, just four months after we met. We got married at a nearby venue (not on top of the mountain). The venue was so beautiful. We wanted our wedding day to be about just the two of us, so we didn't invite anyone. It was one of the best decisions we have ever made. There was not as much pressure as you may have with a traditional big wedding. I wore a beautiful white slim designer wedding gown, and Clint wore his Army dress blues. He looked so handsome! Our wedding photos were amazing. By the way that the photographer positioned themselves to take the pictures, you couldn't tell that there were no guests present at the ceremony. We had an outdoor ceremony and exchanged our vows inside of a beautiful gazebo that was surrounded by a small pond with a swan swimming in it. The "aisle" was a flower-decorated wooden pier that led out the gazebo. Our wedding cake was small and consisted of only the top-tier of a three-tier wedding cake, and we experienced our first dance together as a married couple. We did everything that you would expect to see at a traditional wedding, except there were no guests. It may not have been a traditional wedding, but it was the right decision for us. Our wedding day was so memorable, but I would be lying if I told you that even on our special day, that there wasn't a dark cloud looming over us from the fallout of the events that led up to the day.

The following is the wedding day letter that Clint wrote to me, and I will cherish it forever.

Tammy,

I am so excited that the day has come that you will become my amazing and beautiful wife. I want to share a few things from my heart with you on this special day.

I am so thankful for you and look forward to spending my remaining days sharing my life with you. I believe, with all of my heart, that you are a gift from God and an answered prayer. I truly wish that you knew my thoughts and could see my heart about the extent of my love for you.

I desire to be the man that God wants me to be, and as a result, the husband that you need me to be. I will continue to strive toward improving who I am through the power and grace of God.

I want you to feel loved and secure...to experience unwavering trust in me. That you will fully know and understand that my love for you is unconditional, that my intentions toward you will always be good, that I will protect you, that I will place you before anyone else on this earth, and that I will always be beside you.

I love you more each day. It is my desire that we will continuously grow closer and more intimately together. That we will experience marriage as God designed it.

In spite of all my shortcomings, these are the thoughts, feelings, and desires that reside within the deepest parts of my heart. Please be confident in knowing these things today, as we officially join together as one.

I love you...more...and forever!!!!
Clint

Clint and I have had an enormous strain placed on our marriage. The strain is not only due to the events leading up to our wedding with the broken relationships with his youngest two children, but even some leading up until now. It seemed like we were getting hit from every direction. The stress has been almost unbearable at times. I was so happy when I met Clint. I thought that I had not only gained Clint but a complete family. The family life that I thought I was getting wasn't turning out to be that way. I may not have wanted kids of my own, but a "ready-made" family was a blessing to me. Clint's daughter, Rebekah, was unaccepting of me from the day we met; however, his youngest son, Aaron, was initially accepting of me. Within a few weeks, that would change, and he turned against his father and me, as well. The rejection I felt by the two younger kids towards me was like a big sign that read, "You just aren't good enough." The situation devastated Clint and me. It also brought to the surface all of those previous times that I had felt that I was not good enough in the past.

Everyone knew about the fallout: my family, Clint's family, Pastors, members of our church, co-workers, etc. It was embarrassing and humiliating. I felt such shame like I didn't belong and that I was *personally* responsible for destroying a family. These feelings continued for a few years.

Despite the fact there were some happy times, these overwhelming feelings created a dark cloud over our marriage. I *now* know that it wouldn't have mattered what woman Clint chose to be with, I believe there would have been issues. Issues were brewing before I came along. I just didn't know this at the time, and I beat myself up. At the time, I had placed the blame for *all* of our broken relationships entirely upon myself. Sometimes, I would turn on Clint and blame him.

Clint and I decided that when we got married, that I would quit my job. My mom, as well as others, were shocked. They knew I was very independent and *always* had a backup plan. They had never seen me do this before and didn't understand, but it was the best decision for us. I was forty-one when I quit my job, and I had been working since I was sixteen-years-old. I have always said that Clint is the best man I have ever met in my entire life, and that remains true today. Upon meeting Clint, I decided that I no longer needed a "backup plan." However, the stress of a new marriage, strained family relationships (with my mom, Clint's mom, and the two younger kids) was just about insufferable. Not to mention that I was transitioning from working my entire life to not working at all. It gave me plenty of time to think about *everything*. All I did was think, think, and think some more! My mind was constantly spinning, and my anxiety would get out of control at times.

There had never been a period of my life where I had time to process everything that had happened over my lifetime. There were times when I was single, even though I did a good job taking care of myself, that there wasn't the time or the finances for vacations to relax. It just didn't happen. I was always on the go trying to make ends meet, maintaining friendships, and finding love. I may have taken an occasional day off here and there, but certainly nothing lengthy or extravagant.

The best way I can describe it to you is that everything that was going on with me hit me like a ton of bricks. I was so sick and tired of feeling sick and tired. I wanted all of the pain just to go away. Some people may have turned to alcohol or drugs, but not me. I would shop, and I would rage. Shopping was a medicator for me. It made me feel happy and comfortable at the moment. At times, I would also eat to feel comfortable. Other times, I would get so angry that I would go into a full-blown rage. All I knew was that I was angry. I couldn't pinpoint what or who I was angry at or why I just couldn't seem to process my feelings. I didn't know how to get everything out of my system. It eventually got to the point where I was spiraling so out of control that I decided I had to make a change. I had hit rock bottom.

There were times when I felt as if I were not even good enough for Clint. I want to make it clear that Clint has never once made me feel "less than." It was me that thought I was not good enough! Clint would lay down in traffic for me! I have never been treated better by anyone in my entire life. He is everything to me. I would self-sabotage, albeit subconsciously, and do things to undermine our relationship. There is it again, that feeling of not feeling good enough or worthy enough! I have learned that we will act out in life what we *think* we deserve. For the most part, I knew that I deserved to have a happy life with Clint, but I still felt, at times, my inner critical voice was telling me I wasn't good enough. I am a fixer, and I have never been one to give up. I may have been down, but I sure wasn't out!

Chapter 9

Set My Sites on Onsite

I decided to go to a therapeutic retreat center called Onsite in Cumberland Furnace, Tennessee. I told Clint of my desire to go to Onsite, and he fully supported my decision. I had seen guests referred to Onsite and their workshops on numerous episodes of the *Dr. Phil Show*. Part of my reason for wanting to go to Onsite was to deal with my anxiety, codependency, and past trauma. Since part of my anxiety has to do with being anxious while in a car, I felt that I could make the 125-mile trip from Huntsville. I studied their website and then contacted Onsite to find out specific information about their various programs. I filled out the in-depth intake paperwork and submitted it for review. Within a few days, a program coordinator notified me of my acceptance into the Living Centered Program. I was overwhelmed with anxiety, yet super excited at the very same time! My dream of going and spending time at this "heaven on earth" would soon be realized!

Due to my driving and riding anxiety, Clint drove me to Onsite. I was, of course, anxious along the way and had to stop on the side of the road several times to relieve my anxiety and to try to stop panic attacks from coming on. For almost the entire drive, we listened to Christian *WOW Worship* music. One of the songs that I took great comfort in was "Trust in You" by Lauren Daigle. After several hours on the road, which should have only taken about two hours, Clint and I arrived at Onsite.

After getting checked in, I wanted Clint to walk the grounds with me. Here I was a forty-something-year-old grown woman that was terrified of being left alone in this place, like a little girl. That was my inner child speaking to me. It petrified me at the thought of my husband leaving me there for a week. You are required to turn in your cell phone and any other digital devices that you brought with you, and have zero contact with the outside world for an entire week! I will let you in on a little secret that this is a blessing in disguise, and you won't have time for them anyway! In one week, you receive the equivalent of an entire year worth of counseling sessions. There is no wasted time in the schedule, and each day is organized and planned out for you. An average day may include activities such as meditation, yoga, classes, meals, group counseling, team-building activities, and fellowship.

Clint walked around with me on those grounds for two hours! He was so incredibly patient! When I watched him drive off the property, my heart sank a little bit, and even some panic started to set in. Just typing this right now makes me a bit uneasy about reliving the experience, but I feel like an overcomer at the very same time!

In honor of my agreement with Onsite concerning privacy and anonymity, I won't be able to discuss certain details about the program or those persons that attended with me. We were assigned cabins with three people to a room. The guys and girls had separate cabins, and it was strictly forbidden to be inside an opposite sex cabin at any time. I went inside my cabin and put my suitcase and other bags on the first bed located by the door. It wasn't an accident that I chose the bed by the door. Some might view it as an unsafe location, but I saw it as a natural means to escape, if necessary. I can tell you that after meeting my two roommates, I was comfortable with one of them, but not with the other. I will refer to the roommate that I was comfortable with as Charlotte, and the one I wasn't as Heather.

The very first night at Onsite, we had a night of introduction. Everyone in the program gathered in the same large room. We received an introduction to the program and an orientation of the grounds. An interesting note about the anonymity rules at Onsite is that during the introduction, we were informed that participants are not allowed to share certain aspects of personal information with the other participants. For example, we were not allowed to discuss our careers. I loved the anonymity aspect of Onsite because the rules allowed me to feel more comfortable around the other participants and focus entirely on the program activities.

We then went around the room and gave a brief introduction of ourselves and why we came to Onsite. When it was my turn to open my mouth to speak, I was teary-eyed, scared, and anxious. Even though I was emotional while giving my introduction, just by a quick scan of the room and listening to the other participants, I knew I wasn't alone in these feelings. There were approximately fifty of us who participated in the program. Onsite divided this large group into smaller groups of about ten persons each. Some of the planned activities were with everyone, and others were with your small group.

At the closing of the first night of large group activities, I went back to my cabin with my roommates, Charlotte and Heather. It was lights out for everyone, as we were all nervous about officially starting the program the next day. It is very dark inside the cabins with all of the lights off. As you know, the night-time and darkness have always made me scared to a certain degree. Panic started to set in. I was thinking as I lay in my bed, "What did I just decide to take on by coming here?" "What in the world was I thinking?" "How am I even going to get through the night?" Things continued to get progressively worse.

As I was attempting to fall asleep, Heather said she was going to take a shower. I didn't think anything of it, at least not at the time she told me. As I lay in my bed, attempting to get some sleep, Heather emerged from the bathroom and climbed into bed. The next thing I knew, Heather was right next to my bed, messing around near my suitcase and bags on the floor. She scared the life out of me!

I decided that under no circumstances was I going to stay in the cabin with Heather. She not only scared the life out of me, but she awoke Charlotte and scared her, as well. I didn't confront her, but I immediately got dressed and left the room to find the night supervisor on duty. You have to know that I was scared and desperate to go outside at night, by myself, to find the night supervisor. It may have been around 11 pm when I left the cabin.

I remembered that during the orientation, we were instructed that if we needed anything during the night, we were to go to the main house. Inside the main house near the kitchen, there was a phone that calls the night supervisor on duty. The night supervisor was Richard. I was ecstatic to have found the phone, but when I picked up the phone, I couldn't get it to work. I later found out that the phone jack wasn't fully connected to the phone. I was thinking, "You have got to be kidding me!" "How am I to get help at this point?" It was then that I remembered that when Richard introduced himself at the orientation, he told us where he would be staying the night. It was in a building located on the far side of the cabins. Fortunately for me, it was not too far away from my cabin.

I soon found my way to the building, but I noticed that the side I initially walked up to didn't have a door, but there was a window. I looked down on the ground, and I saw what was probably a mouse or a frog in the shadows. I don't care for either one, but it didn't matter at the time. It was not going to keep me from finding Richard! There was total darkness all around. The only light was from the porch lights located at each cabin. There were a couple of dusk-to-dawn lights for the employee parking lot and the main house, but they didn't provide me much light since they were too far off in the distance or were on the opposite side of the building. One of the men's cabins was right next to the building. I was thinking, "Do I want to possibly cause a commotion by knocking on this window and wake everyone up?" I decided that I had to do what I had to do, at this point! I knew that no matter what happened, I wasn't going back to my assigned cabin.

I thought, "So here goes nothing!" I began knocking on the window. Initially, there was no response from Richard, so I kept knocking and knocking until I finally heard Richard say, "Just a minute." To my relief, help was on the way! Richard emerged from around the corner of the building. Richard asked me what was wrong. I told him, "I can't take it anymore! One of my roommates, Heather, has scared me to death, and something is going on with her! I can't take it!" I described to Richard everything that had happened inside the cabin.

Richard explained to me that he had never experienced anything like this at Onsite and that this was an extremely unusual occurrence. I was thinking to myself, "Oh, this would be just my luck, wouldn't it?" Richard stated that he would have to address the situation in the morning with the clinical staff and program leads. He said that he didn't quite know what to do about my sleeping situation in the meantime. I told him that I saw a sofa in the yoga room in one of the other buildings. I asked him if I could stay in that room for the night. He agreed and told me that he wanted me to feel safe and comfortable, but not to let anyone else know that he allowed me to stay in there, as this was an extenuating circumstance, and there was only one sofa! He went to a closet in that building where they kept extra supplies and got me a blanket and pillow. After ensuring that I had everything I needed, Richard locked the doors so no one could get inside. He told me that he would come back first thing in the morning to unlock the doors. Richard promised me that I would be safe and that he wouldn't forget about me since he was responsible for opening all of the doors the following morning throughout the grounds.

I had no idea that this would become one of the longest nights of my entire life! I settled in on the sofa inside the yoga room, as best as I could, but for some reason, I felt most comfortable sitting on the floor and leaning against it. As I sat on the floor, staring at the hallway light shining through the window at the top of the door into the darkness inside the yoga room, panic started to set in. I was thinking, "I am alone and locked in this unfamiliar place all night long with no husband, family, or friends around!" Nothing was familiar, except God! I firmly believe He is the only reason I was able to make it through the night. It was just me, Him, and my thoughts. Trust me, when I say that if I could ever get out of my head, I could make leaps and bounds in my life! As I sat on that floor, I had an extreme panic attack. I sat there, praying continuously for hours. The panic lasted for a while, but it eventually subsided. I began to shake uncontrollably and have tremors like I usually have following a panic attack. These tremors are a sign to me that most of the panic has subsided. When others have seen me have these tremors and it scared them, I would reassure them that it was okay and that I knew the worst part was over!

Eventually, I was able to get about two hours of sleep in the wee hours of the morning. As I woke up, I noticed that Richard had unlocked the building, and I used a bathroom in the hallway to get ready for the day. This bathroom only had a sink and a toilet. I had to take a sink bath! What I mean is that I had to clean up, and even shave my legs using the sink! I was so proud of myself, not for cleaning up in the sink, but because I survived this horrible first night.

Since I didn't have to stay the night in my cabin, I felt safe, especially from Heather! Later that morning, I was informed that the Onsite leadership was aware of and addressing what had happened with Heather in our cabin. I don't know any other details, but I didn't see her anymore by the end of the second day. I was able to pull myself together, at least to the point to make it through the first day of counseling with my large and small groups! So, I thought.

Though I made it through the first night, in hindsight, I believe that I was using the incident with Heather as a reason to give up. I located one of our large group counselors, Angela. We sat down together and talked for a few minutes. She knew I was on the verge of giving up, and my anxiety was beginning to kick back in. I demanded that she get my cell phone, and I had my finger poised above the call button to contact Clint to come to get me. I wanted to go home because this was too difficult. I didn't feel like I was capable of the emotional work that I was doing. I had explained to Angela that I learned about Onsite from watching the *Dr. Phil Show,* and it was my dream to attend the Living Centered Program at Onsite to heal myself emotionally.

I believe it was at this time that Angela asked me about my faith. I revealed to her that I was a Christian. She told me that she was a Christian, as well as a few of the other leaders. She contacted the Clinical Director, Bill, on her phone. Bill spoke with me and told me that he had reviewed my intake paperwork and saw that I struggled with anxiety. Bill informed me that he believed that my anxiety was at play in the situation. After a few more minutes of talking, Angela and Bill convinced me to give back my phone, continue the program, and to "Trust the Process."

God showed up in a *big* way during this time, but I hadn't yet come to that realization. Leading up to my conversation with Angela, she had shared her backstory during a large group session. I was amazed at her vulnerability and willingness to share some painful truths about her life. It made me feel more comfortable to share with her how I felt when we talked. It also helped that Angela's personality reminded me of my Aunt Dianne, which brought me some familiarity and comfort.

For the first few days, I cried uncontrollably. Richard let me sleep on the yoga room couch for the remainder of my stay at Onsite, and I was so grateful! Although I struggled through every day and night, I was able to get a little bit more sleep each night. That wasn't to say that I wasn't sleep-deprived, because I was so tired and miserable that I was to the point of being nauseous! After a few days of being sleep-deprived and being so emotional, I felt I had reached my breaking point and wanted to go home! My small group counselor, Rosanna, thought that I was getting sick due to all of my emotions coming out. At one point, I was so ill that I went to my cabin around lunchtime to rest. I didn't think that I could make it the rest of the day. Someone in my small group told Rosanna, and she came to my cabin to check on me. I constantly felt like I had to vomit, but every time I went to the bathroom, nothing would come out! It was then that Rosanna explained to me that she thought I was getting out all of the emotions that I had pushed down for years. It was like poison in my system!

Angela told me that she noticed me on the very first day while Clint was walking the grounds with me. She said she thought to herself, "That poor *little girl*!" Angela was referring to my inner child, meaning that due to that particular circumstance, I was operating at the emotional level of a little girl and not an adult. She could see that I was scared, and in that instance, it was as if Clint was walking around with a "little" Tammy.

Rosanna convinced me to come back after lunch and join the small group. Everyone in my small group made me feel welcome, that I belonged there, and that I should continue with the process! Though I started to feel a little bit better, I still longed to go home and be back in my familiar surroundings with my husband.

I enjoyed many of the large group sessions, especially the morning sessions that were educational and designed to introduce us to various topics or tools that we would discuss further in our small groups. One of my favorite portions of the day were the daily meditation sessions that immediately following breakfast. It helped me start my day off in a positive way, reduced my anxiety levels, and prepared me for the start of our small group sessions.

During the evenings, there were fun extracurricular activities that helped you get to know the participants that were not in your small group! I had so much fun doing these activities, especially when we would play games. I have always felt young at heart, and I enjoyed all of the team-building exercises that got us out of our comfort zones and helped us to unwind at the end of the day.

One evening, we ended the day by sitting outside beside a bonfire and making S'mores! Here I was, a forty-something-year-old woman and had never eaten S'mores in my life! Everyone was amazed that I had never had one, and after I did, I was the one that was amazed at what I had been missing! Speaking of delicious food, the meals at Onsite were incredible, and most everyone would agree that the mealtimes were one of the best parts of the day. Not only were the gourmet meals delicious, but it provided another opportunity to connect with others. Even though I was sleep-deprived and nauseous, I have rarely felt bad enough in my life that I couldn't eat! My favorite meal was when they served their made-from-scratch Chicken Pot Pie, and the chef was willing to share her recipe with me!

We did numerous exercises and incorporated experiential therapy in our small groups, including role-playing, where people actively played the roles of family members. We learned about family-mapping and how everyone has a backstory that plays a role in how we engage or interact with people. The various classes helped us understand why someone may have done the things they did in life. We learned about how addiction, trauma, tragedies, and other events can affect a person and their family system. We also learned about medicators and coping mechanisms. A whole new world opened up to me! I gained self-awareness and an appreciation of why people may do what they do. I now view the world around me differently than I did before the program.

I will use one part of my Granddaddy's backstory as an example. The fact that his father was an alcoholic would absolutely shape the way Granddaddy handled things his entire life. I am not saying that what Granddaddy did was good or bad, and I am not speaking about any specific event. I am merely saying that having an alcoholic father alone would impact the way he lived his life, how he coped with things or did *not* cope with things. Everyone has a backstory. Your backstory is a "map" to help us know where we came from, so you can figure out where you need to go in your recovery.

It would be true of any trauma that Grandmama, Mawmaw, and others in my family experienced during their lives. It is true for me, you, and everyone else! Everything counts, even when the trauma was due to no fault of their own. I learned that you don't have to know someone personally to understand that unresolved trauma will present itself in their behavior, and it can be unresolved for a multitude of reasons. It might be that they don't recognize or acknowledge it, help may not have have been available, or they have chosen not to deal with it for whatever reason. These are just a few, but that is the point. It is unresolved for a *reason*. Knowing this *now* allows me to see others and their behavior in a different light. Their behavior may be unacceptable and require that I set a boundary to protect myself, but it also allows me to be more understanding and empathetic.

Now that I have seen what Onsite and therapy has done in my life, it pains me to know that some refuse help. You can't just "get over" trauma. Sometimes, people fear the stigma that is associated with counseling or therapy. They believe others will view them as weak or broken. Others may not want to face their supposed "demons" or the "skeletons in the closet." My personal experience tells me that it takes way more courage, toughness, and determination to face and resolve your trauma than to leave it unresolved. I tend to believe that when I hear someone say that they "don't need help," they may be the very ones that need it the most. There are no truer words than these: Hurt people, hurt people!

One of the highlights of my stay was when we went on a labyrinth walk during one of the morning sessions. I had never heard of this before I attended Onsite. It is an ancient practice for spiritual centering and prayer, where you slowly walk through the labyrinth to quiet your mind and focus on prayer. When you get to the center of the walk, you can, if wish to do so, drop off any "items" you wish to leave there. During my labyrinth walk, it began misting rain, which made the walk just that much more special to me! I felt His presence and comfort. The Bible often refers to rain as a blessing, and I was undoubtedly blessed that morning! While some may say that the rain was a coincidence, I disagree. I've heard it said that coincidence is when God chooses to remain anonymous, and I believe that is true.

During my small group sessions, which lasted throughout the whole day, I would learn and feel like I was becoming a part of the deep-seated emotions and issues of others. What I mean by this is that there is somewhat of an "inside joke," that is actually a truth, that you are not actually at Onsite only for yourself, you are there for others, too. It was a "light bulb" moment for me when I heard it said, "You just thought you came here for *you,* didn't you?" The truth was that all the while that I thought I was alone, I wasn't, and neither was anyone else! They say that "nothing is coincidental" at Onsite, and I believe it with all of my heart. There is a reason for their processes at Onsite. We heard over and over to "Trust the Process!"

I would sit in my small group and listen to the resulting heartache related to drug abuse, loneliness, infidelity, betrayal, shame, physical abuse, or guilt. We would eventually learn that a common underlying theme that a significant number of us in the program shared were characteristics of codependency. Our codependency may have evolved differently, taken different forms, and been at various stages, but the symptoms and behaviors were present. Some people were addicted to alcohol or drugs. My addiction was people, meaning that I was *addicted* to getting my self-worth from others. I didn't know who I was as a person.

My whole life, I was too busy either asking everyone else who I was or believing who everyone said I was! As a person in my early forties, this was a defining moment in my life! I was still operating at a much younger age emotionally. I was walking around as my inner child. I would later go on to learn more about this inner child at Onsite. I also learned that not everyone that comes from a dysfunctional family develops codependency, but codependents do come from a dysfunctional family system. Someone once said, "Anyone that breathes air would benefit from this place!" and they would be correct!

After six days of riding an emotional rollercoaster, where I had experienced everything from panic to peace, rage to calm, crying to laughter, and loneliness to connection, I completed the Living Centered Program at Onsite. There were times that I felt as if this had been the longest week of my entire life, but other times it felt like time flew by. I am so grateful that God was with me every step of the way, and He gave me the strength and endurance I needed to finish. One of the scriptures that gave me strength and confidence throughout my time at Onsite was, *"For I can do everything through Christ, who gives me strength." (Philippians 4-13 – NLT)*

On the last day, our large group met one final time. We each had an opportunity to share what we had experienced over the previous week. It was such an emotional experience, not only when I spoke, but to hear everyone share how the program had impacted them personally. It was amazing to see the difference six days made from the first time we sat together and shared during the introductions about why we *thought* we had come to Onsite, to this closing session. We were all in the same program, yet our journeys were unique to each of us.

During my time to share, I explained that anytime I wanted to "give up" during my stay that it was just the enemy trying to keep me down and trying to steal (John 10:10) from me what God had intended. God was the reason why and how I made it through the program. I shared the point when I was so scared that I had demanded that the staff get my phone, and I had my finger on the button to call Clint! Thank goodness I changed my mind. My life was forever changed! I believe that my decision to stay was God's plan for me! I had to experience everything I did to come out on the other side changed. My tears that day were partly due to the struggle that I just experienced, yet joyful at "pushing the reset button" and starting my "new" life!

The closing ceremony was a special time for me. It was a time of reflection of everything that had happened the previous week and the excitement of reuniting with Clint. The CEO of Onsite, Miles Adcox, attended our closing ceremony. He spoke to us for a few minutes and watched us graduate from the program. Following the closing ceremony, I had the opportunity to go around the room and thank each of the staff members and hug them! Miles was first, followed by Bill, Rosanna, and the remainder of the Living Centered Program counselors and staff. When I found Richard, I thanked him for letting me stay on the couch each night. He embraced me with a big hug and said, "I just wanted you to be comfortable!"

At this point, during the closing ceremony, I knew Clint was already waiting outside to pick me up. Now keep in mind that I had not seen or spoken to him in a week. As soon as the double barn doors opened, I sprinted, and I do mean I sprinted towards him waiting by the car and jumped up in his arms! I will never forget it! I couldn't wait to share with him everything that I had learned and overcome with God's help and guidance.

I never imagined that I would have experienced this much love and connection in such a short time! All of us were strangers, all of us on our journeys, all of us wrestled with our emotions, yet we were committed to each other throughout the process, be it only for a week. One of the most impactful moments for me was during one of our large group session exercises. We arranged enough chairs for half of us to sit down in a circle. Half of us sat down in the chairs, and the other half stood behind someone in a chair. Those who were standing leaned down in our ear and whispered something that they wished that they had heard growing up. Then they rotated around the room until they had shared it with everyone sitting down. Once the rotation was complete, we switched roles. I will tell you that I have never experienced anything like it, nor had I ever been so emotionally moved by anything close to this experience in my entire life! You would have to experience it firsthand to grasp the *love* that was present in the room. To say that I felt like I had a new life after Onsite, would be an understatement.

When I jumped in Clint's arms after the closing ceremony, we held each other for at least a couple minutes. I told him that I wanted him to meet a few people inside. I was so happy that Clint got to meet Rosanna, Richard, the other staff, and everyone in my small group. About six months later, Clint and I went back to Onsite to attend the Coupleship Program. It was a challenging but wonderful time spent with other couples. We were able to meet and make lifelong friends with one of the couples, Diana and Bobby.

Not long after completing the Coupleship Program, Clint was able to participate in the Veteran's Living Centered Program. Upon arriving at Onsite, and before the opening ceremony to turn in his cell phone, Clint saw Rosanna. In passing, Rosanna told Clint to tell me, "You be sure to send her my love, love, love!" I was excited that Clint was able to experience the program that made such a positive impact on my life. One of the hardest things to do was to not share my experience at Onsite with Clint prior to him attending his program, as it would take away from his experience. I will say that these experiences at Onsite changed both of our lives forever. It indeed was like a slice of heaven on earth!

Chapter 10

I Must Be Doing Something Right

Thank you for following along as I shared my backstory and the beginnings of my recovery process. The following are *my* thoughts on *key lessons* that I have learned during my recovery journey. Allow me to begin by providing some additional contextual information.

For many years, when I tried to talk to Mom about certain things that she would do that hurt me, it was met with contempt, denial, or deflection. She would usually counter my complaint or feelings with something that she had done that *was* good in my life. However, that wasn't the point. The point was the *issue* that I was trying to discuss with her. There were times that she would make me feel shameful over things I would or would not do. There was a lot of stonewalling and a lot of defensiveness. Some of this is a very natural reaction. I explain all of this to paint a picture for you of *how* and *why* I felt the way that I *used* to feel about her.

Often, my mom would make it a point to tell me how *different* I was from the rest of the family. She would say to me that I was too confrontational when most of my family likes to keep the peace. She would especially remind me of this before seeing our family at different functions. I eventually asked her why she would say this to me. She said she didn't say it to hurt my feelings. I'm *not* saying that what she said about me wasn't true at the time. However, the criticism and resulting shame were unbearable to me. No one wants to hear these types of comments from their mother, especially when I felt that I didn't receive what I truly needed from her.

I vowed to myself that I would *never* be shamed again for anything, or live feeling like I was not good enough, I am enough, just the way I am! There were plenty of times that I talked to her about other things and people in my life. She was often helpful, but we just couldn't seem to speak about matters concerning us. My relationship with my mom was the most *crucial* and the most *damaged* one in my life.

One of the things I have always desired is to feel that my mom completely accepted me for who I am and for her to validate my feelings. The opposite of this is a *fear* of rejection and abandonment. This fear plays an enormous part in my interactions and relationship with my mom. Regardless of *who* it is with, when there is conflict, I want to tackle it head-on and put it to rest. Unresolved conflict can exacerbate my anxiety. If I allow myself, I will ruminate on the situation until I have a panic attack!

My mom is much less direct and doesn't like conflict. She is a passive person that tends to shut down and withdraw. I understand that this is a difference in personality. However, my mom's avoidance of conflict can result in her burying things and not wanting to come back around to discuss and work through our differences. This dynamic created an environment for a vicious cycle that I refer to as the "crazy train." The crazy train would arrive, and the two of us would hop on for the ride!

A crazy train ride looks like this: My mom and I would have a disagreement and argue. We would lash out and verbally abuse one another. My mom would get upset with me and shut down. She would refuse to speak with me and cut off the relationship. Sometimes, this would be for extended periods. When she would do this, it created fear and panic inside of me! I would be overwhelmed with anxiety, due to my fear of being rejected and abandoned by my mom. So much so, that I would have panic attacks. Some of which required a trip to the emergency room. While she was not talking to me, she would do things that I would *interpret* as being passive-aggressive. It felt like she was *intentionally* trying to *punish* me since she knew how devastated I was with her cutting off the relationship. Her silence and passive-aggressiveness would only further add fuel to the fire because I would make attempts to *force* her to talk to me or call her out on her passive-aggressive behavior. If she didn't (or did) respond, I would rage and say hurtful things. Doing this only further separated us. This loop could occur several times during a *single* argument.

I cannot recall a single incident when this cycle would occur that my mom reached out to me to reconcile. When my mom would be ready to reconnect, she usually wouldn't want to talk about what had happened. It forced me to push down not only my feelings from the previous argument but all of the feelings and anxiety I experienced *while* she had cut me off from the relationship. As a result, the next argument wasn't just about the matter at hand, but it would be about the matter at hand, *plus* everything else that I had been forced to push down. It would *all* come back out during the next cycle because it had never been resolved, nor could we resolve it in a healthy manner.

This vicious cycle has played out over-and-over again throughout my entire life. My recovery has provided me with *awareness*. It has allowed me to understand why this pernicious cycle occurred and to accept my mom, and myself, for who and where we are at any given time. This awareness and understanding helps me to allow the crazy train to continue rolling past me. I have a *choice* to either hop on, knowing the consequences, or allow it to pass me by and maintain my peace and serenity.

During my recovery, I shared some of my counseling and recovery experience with my mom. Part of me wishes that I had never done this because it usually made matters worse. I feel that when I was sharing my work with her, a part of me was still seeking validation and acceptance from my mother. Often, I didn't receive validation and acceptance, but I did receive an invitation for a ride on the crazy train. Sadly, there were times I hopped on board.

I would share information and stories with my mom about what I was working through and learning in my counseling sessions. There were times when I spoke about an event or a particular topic that would be a trigger for her. She would get upset and become defensive. Do you hear the train whistle blowing? She would say things, such as, "How did you have a bad childhood?" "You didn't starve, and you had a roof over your head!" "You blame me for everything!" "You need help and medication!" There were times that I *chose* not to jump off the train when she would say these types of comments, and I would lash out and verbally abuse her.

It may sound obvious, but I learned a hard lesson that when someone has not experienced therapy for themselves, then there is a good possibility that they will not understand. It is naturally going to seem confusing *why* we do the things we do in therapy. I *wanted* her to understand and *wanted* her to be proud of me for all of the difficult inner emotional work I was doing in therapy. What she was not hearing me say was that my childhood was filled with a *combination* of good and bad events. I wasn't saying that my childhood was *all* bad, but people don't seek counseling for the "good" parts of their life. I was seeking help to work through those "bad" times to heal. Therefore, those events *were* the focus during my sessions. For the most part, these conversations where I was trying to *explain* my therapy only served to damage my recovery process and our relationship further.

It is my honest belief that my mother thought that I would do my recovery work and come out "fixed." I'm sure she is not alone in this belief. I wish it were that easy. One fallacy in this way of thinking is that we are all imperfect persons. Recovery is about *progress* and not *perfection*. I am 100 percent responsible for *me*, and no one else gets to define what is best for me. This is precisely why my recovery must continue, meaning the process is never complete. Again, I wholeheartedly believe that a part of me was still seeking validation and acceptance from my mother. I had to come to grips and accept that there are some things that she may never be able to give me. This is one of the hardest lessons that I have learned during my recovery process. I had been spinning my wheels for years, trying to gain the necessary traction to move forward for something that may never happen. During recovery, I learned *how* I could give these things to myself.

There may be people reading this book that would say that the Bible says to honor your father and your mother. However, it also addresses abusive relationships and protecting yourself from abuse. Many people struggle with honoring their father and mother for a multitude of reasons. I am not referring to parents that act honorably, and their children are rebellious. Many people have parents, if they even know who they are, that abused, neglected, or abandoned them. This is why I say that many people struggle with this Commandment.

I feel that *I do* know what it takes to be a parent, which is one of the *very* reasons why I chose never to be one. Trust me, I'm judged for choosing not to be a parent. "What's wrong with her?" "That's just not natural!" "How could she be so selfish?" Those that think or say these things shouldn't judge and don't get to take my inventory. Instead, they should be seeking an understanding of *why* people do the things they do, rather than making a judgment based upon assumptions or lack of information. There is a reason why the following saying exists, "No one has walked a mile in my shoes!" It's because no one can fully understand or grasp what someone else is going through or has gone through in their life. You may be able to empathize with them, but you will never truly understand. Even though I chose not to be a mother, I still have motherly instincts. No doubt, in my mind, had I decided to be a mother *after* I received help, I would have been a great one.

There may be some that would say, "How could she have felt that way about her mother and father?" First, no one *wants* the feel this way about their parents. I would also say that just because someone owns a title, such as, mom, dad, brother, sister, friend, boss, etc., does not give that person the right to behave in a way that is harmful to someone and expect that person to accept it as being okay. What they should expect is a boundary placed to prevent further abuse. Some people will use these titles or roles as justification for their poor or abusive behavior, and then *they* get upset when a boundary is placed by the person they are abusing.

When I hear someone say, "Just get over it!" I simply say, "Bless your heart." They don't understand that you are not able to *heal* from trauma without adequately addressing it. The trauma may get buried, but it is still there and will show itself in other ways until it's properly healed. You cannot *think* your way out of trauma.

Please don't misinterpret what I am saying. I'm *not* saying that you shouldn't forgive the abuser. You absolutely should forgive! However, that forgiveness is more beneficial for you and your health, than for the abuser. You can forgive someone while placing a boundary to prevent further abuse. Just because you set a boundary does not mean that you have not forgiven the abuser. It means that you love yourself enough to protect yourself from further abusive behavior while forgiving the abuser.

One might say, "Well, she is just an angry person!" Yes, I *was* angry. It happened, and I have nothing to hide. I will admit that I said many things to hurt others, especially my mother and father, to inflict pain on them just like I felt they did to me. Over and over, time and time again, I have said some ruthless things and acted out in ways that I am not proud of toward others. I own my portion, 100 percent. This behavior was unacceptable. However, one must ask themselves, "*Why* did she behave this way?" There are numerous factors and variables involved in answering this question. It would undoubtedly take more than one book to cover it all. I have done my best to give you an inside glimpse of my life, so you would be able to answer that question. I intentionally left out events in my life, either due to personal reasons or relevance to the reader.

I spoke earlier about recovery providing me with a better *awareness* of myself, particularly my emotions. I have learned in therapy that anger is a *secondary* emotion. Anger is a result of someone feeling fear, sadness, or hurt. Knowing this, when I recognize or become *aware* that I am becoming angry, I ask myself *why* I'm feeling angry. I must dig deeper to understand.

Another example is that I have become aware of and look for what I call "masks." A mask is when I feel emotions and/or respond to someone *as if* they are someone else that caused me trauma. For example, I am interacting with someone, and they do or say something that triggers an emotional response due to past trauma in my life. When this happens, I must be *aware* enough not to elicit a response toward the person I'm interacting with as if they are the person, or mask, that caused the trauma. I have heard these triggers referred to as "landmines" because when someone steps on the landmine, it causes an emotional explosion. I must be aware of my landmines, and when one is triggered, so I can control my responses. My therapist explained to me that it is a good idea for people, especially those in a close relationship, to know each other's landmines, so you don't step on one.

Through my recovery, I *now* understand that these factors and variables did not justify *why* I behaved the way I did toward others. I am responsible and accountable for my actions. I was not a victim or powerless in my situation. Those that hurt me were not horrible people whose sole purpose in life was to harm me. Simply put, we were all hurt and therefore hurting others, because we had not healed from our trauma.

Not only have I endured and lived everything that you have read thus far in this book, but I had to relive the hurtful parts again while writing this book. I have learned that being vulnerable in this way takes courage. If this book impacts the life of only one person, it was worth it to me. The world is changed, one person at a time. There were times I had to stop writing because of being temporarily overwhelmed with emotion. I shed a lot of tears recalling some of the stories I've shared, but I experienced great joy and happiness with others.

The good news is that my recovery has made me, well, a better me! The worst is behind me since I have learned *how* to heal from my trauma. I know that there will be traumatic events in my future, but *now* I know what I must do to heal. I understand the process, and that brings me great peace in having this knowledge. Grace and forgiveness are expected not only of me but for the ones that have contributed to my life in negative ways. That is the way I *try* to live my life today. No, it's not always easy, and I'm certainly far from perfect, but when I do apply what I have been taught during recovery and emplace necessary boundaries, it sure makes things go a lot smoother.

I would have been doing myself a vast injustice, as well as others, if I had stayed "stuck" and reverted to living my life the way I did before I began my recovery. It wasn't my fault about the things that happened to me at any point in my childhood, but it was my responsibility to do something about it as an adult. I am very proud of myself, and I'll never be the same. Thank you, God, for leading me, and giving me the strength, determination, and hope I needed to be healed through your touch and my recovery process!

For many of us, we are not close to some of our immediate family. It may be just a matter of different personalities. Sometimes there are outside influences that have contributed to the family dynamics. In my opinion, there are no easy answers in these situations.

The relationship with my dad is still distant, but better nonetheless. We can never get lost time from the past back, nor do I truly believe we ever bonded like a father and daughter should have bonded. What I do believe is that I "dodged a bullet" for many years by *not* having my dad in my life and that it was indeed a blessing in disguise. I know how it sounds, and I don't like admitting it, but for many years he was broken and hurting. To some degree, he still is, but since giving his life to Christ years ago, my father is not the same man he used to be. I have empathy because I accept that he is doing the best that he can, based upon his circumstances.

I've learned that people cannot give you what they do not possess themselves. This one aspect is an example of why recovery can be so hard. I had to develop unconditional acceptance of my dad for *who* he is, and *where* he is, at this moment. If he cannot be the father I desire him to be, then I must accept that he cannot be that person at this moment. It's not that he can't be at some point in the future, but that it is not where he is today. I had to grieve that loss of a father that I so desired and ultimately come to acceptance at the end of the grieving process. This grieving process has been one of the most challenging things I've had to do during my recovery. This unconditional acceptance applies to everyone, including an unconditional acceptance of myself. The unconditional acceptance of myself is the first step to being able to provide unconditional acceptance to others. Again, we cannot give to others that which we don't possess ourselves!

There is so much that I don't understand about my parents. I have questioned things my entire life. To say that I have lived most of my life having trust issues, would be an absolute understatement. Every person that has had an intimate relationship with me throughout my life has paid a certain price for choosing to be with me. I say that to demonstrate to you how trauma causes a ripple effect. Maybe it isn't meant to be that I have all the answers. I understand and accept that because I believe that God knows what is best for me. I love my mother, and though I may not always agree with her, I do try to respect her. For the most part, I believe that she loves and respects me. My mom has told me during my recovery that I blame her for *everything!* Again, this is incorrect! She would say this when I would naturally try to hold her accountable for her wrongdoing during my childhood.

I do believe that for many years, it was easier to blame her for a lot of the things that I did not have because my dad wasn't in the picture. I think this was unfair to her. However, I felt at the time I was growing up, that I looked to her to provide me with emotional support, in addition to other things she provided, *since* my dad wasn't in the picture. I do appreciate everything she did for me, and I now recognize that she did the best she could at the time. It doesn't change the resulting pain I felt from not having the emotional support I desperately needed, but just like my dad, my mom couldn't give me the things that she did not possess herself.

I was thinking about these things, mostly as a child, and when I was emotionally immature. Now, that isn't to say that I don't believe that my mom could have been there more for me because she could have been. What is important to me *now* is that she has fully acknowledged her shortcomings, and I accept that she did the best she could. Acknowledging is only the first step. The next step is that she, along with my dad, do their best not to *continue* doing the same behaviors that have hurt me in the past. I have had to establish boundaries to protect myself from being hurt while allowing them to be who they are in our relationship. These boundaries have created limitations on how intimate our relationship can be, but that is something I have had to accept.

My understanding is that the best role model for a child is the same same-sex parent. From my perspective, it was tough to hear my mom's criticism and to feel the pain and resentment I had for so many years toward her. The biggest kicker is that no one *wants* to feel the way I *used* to feel about their mother. No one! Imagine what it was like for me to be living with this inner turmoil for so many years.

How exactly do my mother and I get along now? We simply don't discuss the hurtful past! We have proven time and time again that we cannot discuss our past issues or any emotions associated with it. Therefore, we cannot discuss any new events that would require a conversation on a deeper or emotional level. I've accepted that we may never be able to have these types of discussions, and this boundary allows us to maintain a relationship that is free of toxicity.

What I am ultimately trying to say is that even though I don't agree with everything my parents have done or didn't do, I try not to judge them and have more empathy for them *now*. Doing this allows me to stay "centered" and "balanced." It would not have been possible without God, and the myriad of resources, such as, Onsite, counselors, mentors, CoDA meetings, and certain family and friends that have assisted me along my journey.

Some might say, "Well, you don't know my situation, Tammy, and I don't know if I can forgive." All I ask you to do is to try. God forgave us, and He calls us to extend grace and forgiveness to others, as well. Forgiveness is for *you* and not the other person. It doesn't release them from any wrongdoing. I know all about forgiveness because I forgave a man that could have potentially ended my life before it even began. I had to forgive a woman that I should have been able to count on more than anyone else. I had to forgive many other people in my life that have done and said hurtful things to me over the years, and others have forgiven me. I decided to forgive so that we might enjoy the rest of our lives in peace with one another.

Remember the ripple effect! The broken relationships that I had with my parents affected other people, especially other close family members. It's not just about us. I go where God leads me, and I believe he led me here where I am today, writing my story for a reason. My story isn't over yet! I call my book *Anxiously Freed* because I am freed from the bondage. I have lived over half of my life as an anxious person, and I can tell you that doing my recovery work and seeking help has severely reduced my anxiety.

I will never have kids of my own, especially at this point in life. I have also heard that parenting doesn't come with an instruction manual. No, I don't believe that I deserved what I got or didn't get from my parents, but again, they couldn't give me what they didn't possess themselves. I'm not saying that they are *fully* responsible for all of my life up until now. I certainly have taken ownership of *my part* of the things that have happened in my life. What I am saying is that I didn't get to my trauma all by myself. If I didn't mention the very hurtful and painful events involving my relationships, I would be lying and deceiving you. It also wouldn't be as effective in helping others that have gone through similar life events. I hope that you have been able to relate to some part of my story and realize that hope and help are abundant from God and that there are quality resources available to assist you in your journey.

The idea here is not to portray myself as a victim but to simply tell my story. I am not a victim, but a survivor and overcomer! There are many twists and turns to my story. What I do know is that God said he would restore what has been taken from me in this life. *"God, your God will restore everything you lost; he'll have compassion on you; he'll come back and pick up the pieces where you were scattered." (Deuteronomy 30:3 - MSG)*

One of the things that they tell you at Onsite is that the aftercare, upon completion of a program, is absolutely crucial! Aftercare means that you follow-up with a counselor in your local community to continue working on the foundation established at Onsite. Onsite is not a cure-all, and if you don't have a counselor, Onsite will assist you in locating one that can help you in your aftercare. It doesn't mean that you won't struggle when you go back home and enter back into the life and routine you left before Onsite. You should expect to have struggles and possibly significant struggles. You are returning to the very same environment that led you to attend an Onsite program! No one is saying if you went to Onsite and completed a program, that it wouldn't help you. However, if you don't go home and do your "homework" as I like to call it, it won't be nearly as effective.

I immediately decided that when I got home that I was going to complete my aftercare and continue my counseling work. Not only did I do this, but I began searching for a Christian counselor that specialized in the areas that were critical to my recovery. I tried multiple counselors before I found one that was a good fit for me. Additionally, I discovered that a psychologist was extremely valuable for portions of my recovery. Keep an open mind and explore all of your options to find what works best for you and your recovery.

I even started to go to meetings specifically geared towards codependency. I did intense personal work for a couple of years. It was during this time in the midst of having several resources providing me with different types of "help" that I became confused from all of the information swimming around in my head. In my mind, I was looking for *the* solution, when in reality, the various resources were providing me their opinion. There is no such thing as a one-size-fits-all solution in recovery. Sure, there are basic guidelines or rules, but each person has a unique journey.

One common theme I can tell you that I received from all of these resources is this: Learning to love myself. Despite what many may think, I had never done this in my life! I can honestly say that it wasn't until my forties that I even started to understand what it meant "to truly love myself." I am speaking about a healthy love for yourself, not a conceited type. I don't mean walking around saying to yourself, "I have my stuff together, and you don't!" That is self-righteous thinking. Sure, we are all selfish at times. However, what I learned is that self-care and being selfish is not the same thing!

Other than God, I am the only one that has been with me through every moment of my entire life from birth until now, and I am the only person that will be with me 100 percent of the time from this point until He brings me home for eternity! It is true for you, as well! If you don't love yourself for who you are, this earthly life is going to be a long and hard road. The point is that unconditional love for ourselves is foundational, and we must do whatever it takes to learn to love ourselves unconditionally and take care of ourselves.

When you marry, part of your marriage vows includes, "forsaking all others." Yes, I'm absolutely joined together with Clint as one. However, it doesn't mean that I am not a completely separate person from my spouse because I am. My point is that we each had, have, and will continue to have separate and distinct feelings about things and situations. Despite my former marriages, I take my wedding vows with Clint very seriously. Forsaking *all* others does mean *all* others. Everyone, no matter what! That requires telling people "no" at times. Sometimes, it is difficult for people to tell others no, even when it is to their detriment. Telling someone that you can't do something is okay. I've had to remind myself of this many times. It comes back to taking care of yourself, and asking if whatever they are requesting is in your best interests or within your ability to do. At times, we can easily find ourselves overcommitting to even *good* things. Overcommitting ourselves can take a toll on our health, and may even turn into resentment. Neither is good, and it is due to our inability to say one simple word, "No!"

One of the many things taught in therapy is boundaries. Boundaries are to protect yourself. If you place a boundary for punishment, that is manipulation, not a boundary! One of the hardest boundaries or situations where I have had to tell someone "no" has been in the church. We, as Christians, still need to have boundaries. Unfortunately, both inside and outside of the church, some people will try to manipulate you, in the name of Jesus, to try to get you to do something, especially if they would benefit from it. Now, don't misunderstand what I am saying here, as I believe in helping people and serving where you are led. I am merely saying that people will take advantage of you in this world, especially when they have a stake in the matter, Christian or not. It can and does happen in relationships unrelated to people of faith. One example of this is what I've mentioned previously, where someone believes that just because they possess a particular title or role, that they feel that they are entitled to certain things. This behavior is unacceptable and is a form of manipulation.

Previously, I had stated that you must love and take care of yourself. The Bible says to love your neighbor as yourself. Who comes *first* in that verse?

You come first, and it goes back to self-care. Self-care is not selfish, and you must do it! Doing what is genuinely best for you *is* loving yourself. If you don't love yourself or practice self-care, it is impossible to love your neighbor. There was a time that my "neighbor" would not have wanted me to love them as I loved myself. I didn't love myself, and to be honest, I didn't even like myself! Would you have wanted me to treat and love you how I was treating myself? No, I don't think you would.

Something else that self-care does is that it sometimes forces others to take care of their "own" issues. It allows everyone else to take care of themselves. As a codependent, I would sometimes try to "fix" someone else's problem, when it is their problem to handle. The only person I can change is myself! Self-care will also help keep you from being manipulated. You are not the one that is selfish. If someone is trying to manipulate you, that is selfishness on *their* part!

Another aspect of self-care is what I have learned as the five gifts: See what you see, feel what you feel, think what you think, do what you do, and be who you are. These are gifts for you, and you should give these gifts to others by letting them do the same. There is no reason to feel guilt or shame when you practice self-care. You must do what is right for you, as you are ultimately the only one that is going to be there with you throughout this life, besides God. That is the very essence of being your own best friend.

I want to pass on a bit of advice that I always try to remember, and that is, "I don't have to participate in every argument that I have been invited to join." Yes, you heard me correctly. We *don't* have to participate, and we *do* have a choice. A boundary should be emplaced or enforced. If you feel you are in a situation or conversation that is not emotionally safe, you simply cease any further discussion at that moment by saying something as simple as, "This isn't working for me." That protects you 100 percent. The other party may get upset or angry, but you are doing what you need to do to take care of yourself.

Many people make the mistake of thinking that they can talk to others, as a way to work things out or convince them of our viewpoint. It is not always the case. If you are talking to a person that is not healthy or emotionally safe for you, you may potentially cause more damage and pain than if you didn't engage in the conversation. This advice was a significant learning point for me and one of the most challenging things for me to implement. I believed that I could get the "light bulb" to go off in someone's head, or that I could make them "get it." It usually backfired, as it is not my role to *fix* them or make them *get it*. If I am honest with myself, I was usually trying to *change* them or *force* my viewpoint, when my focus should have been on changing me! When I apply this one concept, my relationships improve and is just one more reason why my recovery has been life-changing. I now understand that if a person is not healthy or emotionally safe, then not engaging with them is what is safest for me. It is not my responsibility to "fix" or "change" people, and not engaging someone prevents me from getting "sucked in" to a harmful conversation.

You have to look at people's motivation and intent, and not just rely on black and white thinking. I feel that empathy is essential. Empathy is *not* sympathy! They are two different things, and many people confuse the two. I honestly don't believe that I was truly able to have empathy towards others until I went to Onsite, and I started doing my recovery work as a part of my counseling and therapy. It took me over forty years to become who I was, and "fixing" the toxic person that I *was* would take some time. I am not saying that it would take forty more years, but I am saying to give yourself a break. As they say, "Rome wasn't built in a day!" It takes courage, commitment, and sacrifice. Also, no two journeys are alike!

My psychologist, Dr. Patrick Quirk, PsyD, once told me a personal story about his own family. One day, I was in his office and reminded him of the story. I said, "Do you remember telling me that story about how you and your family only attend your family reunion for three days?" He immediately interrupted and said, "No, Tammy, I said three hours!" We both just laughed! The point is he decided to attend his family reunion once a year to get together with people he loved, but he had to set a boundary. I'm paraphrasing here. He said he would tell his kids in the car what to expect when they arrived. He would say things, such as, "What do we know about Grandma?" "We know that Grandma is sometimes in a bad mood and has little patience." "We want to be kind to Grandma, and we want the time we spend with Grandma to be good, don't we?" It doesn't mean that you are being unfair, mean, or offending someone. It simply means you are taking the steps and doing whatever is necessary to take care of yourself emotionally and allowing others to do the same. We can practice this example with any relationship. Ask yourself ahead of time, "What do we know about so-and-so?" Doing this may help you interact with them more positively.

Upon completion of all the "help" and therapy, and after investing so much in myself, I can't turn back. I don't want to! I didn't do all of this inner emotional work to fall back into being my "old self." I am *enough*, just the way I am. That isn't to say that I won't struggle, as I certainly will. It just means that I am not going to go backward. I can't and shouldn't go back into the toxic environment that made me "sick." I now have an assortment of new tools to handle various situations. Before I began recovery, I used a hammer to fix everything! It was a huge adjustment going from having only my hammer to an entire toolbox.

There were times during recovery that it felt overwhelming. I felt like I was getting hit from every direction. Even with everything I was learning, it was just too much. One day, I decided to "let go and let God," so to speak. I decided to drop all the balls that I had been juggling in the air and let them fall where they may. Asking a person who has struggled with anxiety for most of their adult life to "let go" is almost like asking for the impossible! It takes practice, and often, it is a daily struggle. Anxiety is fear of the unknown. You can tell someone not to worry all day long and not to be afraid. You can even quote your favorites scripture, but if someone doesn't know *how* to do it, it can't easily be done.

I will always be what I refer to as a WIP (Work-In-Progress). To be completely honest with you, just getting by day-to-day is sometimes a significant feat! My work will never be complete. My goal is to live a better life today than I did yesterday. Again, recovery is about *progress*, not *perfection*. I am not competing with anyone. Luckily, life isn't a residual effect. That means that we can pick up right now, where we are in life, and start over. Others may try to keep us stuck where we used to be in life. We may even do self-sabotaging things that will keep ourselves stuck, but it doesn't have to be this way forever. We can start anew every day.

One of the most therapeutic parts of my journey for me was making amends with former friends, enemies, family, and ex-spouses. I reached out and spoke with my former spouses, Chris and Jason. They were both appreciative and expressed their apologies back to me. I cannot fully explain how comforting it is to know that I have done everything that I possibly can to have peace in my heart, regardless of what the other person does with it. Not all of my attempts at making amends were accepted. That's okay because I can only control myself. Does it help that most of the people that I was attempting to make amends with accepted those amends from me? The answer is a resounding, yes!

A lot of us don't always like to talk about God's grace. Why? Because we know that grace doesn't let us "off the hook." *Well then, should we keep on sinning so that God can show us more and more of his wonderful grace?*

Of course not! Since we have died to sin, how can we continue to live in it? (Romans 6:1-2 – NLT) We don't seem to mind talking about God's grace for ourselves, but what isn't easy to talk about is how God requires us to extend it to others! To move forward in our faith, we must let go of what doesn't serve us. We must extend grace to others because God extends it to us every single day. *Bear with each other and forgive whatever grievances you may have against one another. Forgive as the Lord forgave you. (Colossians 3:13 – NIV)* I want to make sure that I don't confuse anyone here. The goal here is to try to make peace and to get along with others. It doesn't mean that we should put ourselves in a toxic situation and not have boundaries with unhealthy people, as I touched on before. Of course, this is a two-way street. I expect that others may have boundaries with me, as well. If two people are toxic and one person receives help, and the other one doesn't, it is *still* a toxic relationship.

At some point during my day, as a part of my prayer time, I ask God for these four things.

1) I pray that I will love and view others as God does and that in turn, others would love me and see me as He does. I'm so thankful for the love of God. Paul described His love for us in this way, *"For I am convinced that neither death nor life, neither angels nor demons, neither the present nor the future, nor any powers, neither height nor depth, nor anything else in all creation, will be able to separate us from the love of God that is in Christ Jesus our Lord." (Romans 8:38-39 – NIV)* Oh, what a different world we would live in if we loved each other as God loves us!

2) I pray that God will help me to accept myself unconditionally, and to remember that just when I think that I can't forgive others that Jesus already paid the price for us and dropped the charges! If we can't accept ourselves and forgive, it is like saying what Jesus did on the cross wasn't good enough, when it was more than good enough, it was *perfect*! Our salvation is a result of His love and His forgiveness for us. He forgave first, so why can't we forgive? We should forgive, and it is commanded of us to do so. *Make allowance for each other's faults, and forgive anyone who offends you. Remember, the Lord forgave you, so you must forgive others. (Colossians 3:13 – NLT)* To be forgiven, we must forgive. Now,

forgiveness doesn't equal restoration. We can forgive, but trusting again can be difficult. I believe we must try because our God is a God of restoration! Frequently, I hear people speak about forgiving themselves. Nowhere in the Bible does it say that we should forgive ourselves. We ask God and others to forgive us.

3) I pray that God will help me live in FAITH (Forsaking All I Trust Him). I use this acronym as a reminder of how I want to live my life. If you are a "control freak," this will be very challenging for you. Sometimes, I will jokingly say that when God passed out patience, he evidently skipped me! Patience is certainly not my strong point. Also, controlling behavior has everything to do with fear. Fear is not what God had intended for us. *Do not be anxious about anything, but in every situation by prayer and petition with thanksgiving, present your requests to God. (Philippians 4:6-7 – NLT)*

4) I pray that God will reveal to me a list of things to be grateful for that day. We all have something to be grateful for, even if it's for the air that we breathe. Maybe it's for all of our unanswered prayers! Things *we* thought *we* wanted, when God's plan for your life, and mine, is far better than anything we could plan for ourselves. *Now all glory to God, who is able, through his mighty power at work within us, to accomplish infinitely more than we might ask or think. (Ephesians 3:20 – NLT)* I have also heard it said, "We plan, and God laughs!" My understanding is that gratitude has been linked to better sleep, reduced stress, better overall health, more personal growth, less negativity, and more energy. It leads to self-acceptance and purpose.

I can tell you that in my own life, just having peace of mind is one of the greatest gifts I can give myself, and I believe that it is for you, as well. They say worry looks back (depression), and fear looks ahead (anxiety) when all we need to focus on is the *now*! None of us are guaranteed tomorrow or even the next minute. I am not suggesting in any way that we should just "wing it." There is nothing wrong with planning, and to a certain degree, I feel that we all must plan for the future. Just not to the point that we aren't truly living in the moment. Today is a gift! Before I roll out of bed each morning and my feet hit the floor, I pray, "God, thank you for today, and help me use this gift wisely."

I still struggle with my driving and riding anxiety. I have to get out on the road and "practice." Practicing on the interstate isn't exactly easy! I also still struggle with social anxiety. Anyone with anxiety knows that you have what I call "board meetings" in my head. It is common to have these at 2:00 a.m. What does a board meeting look like, you ask? It is waking up for no apparent real reason and thinking, "Did I turn off the oven?" "What if what I said to Susie earlier today sounded insensitive?" "I hope I get some sleep tonight, and I am not late for my meeting in the morning!" "Man, that tie that Joe was wearing yesterday sure did look hideous!" "I should have turned the ceiling fan on high." "Do I have to get up and use the bathroom again?" "Should I have shared my opinion in Sunday school yesterday?" "I knew it was going to be a bad day when I forgot to put my deodorant on!" "I need to bathe the dogs this weekend." "I sure have gained a lot of weight!" "Did I pay the electric bill?" These types of random thoughts just continue spinning in my head during a 2:00 a.m. "board meeting"! Would you like me to send you a meeting invite?

Friends, this is just a *glimpse* into anxiety. You just can't tell someone not to worry. Oh, how I wish it were that easy! Now, I am not saying that if you have thoughts like these, that you have anxiety, but what I am saying is that a person that struggles with anxiety and codependency is just about guaranteed to have thoughts like these. We all struggle with some traits and characteristics that could fall into the category of codependency, but that doesn't mean you are a full-blown codependent. If you are truly a codependent, understand that there is help out there for you.

Similar to divorce, some will place a stigma on seeking mental health treatment, even within the church. I am thankful for and blessed with Pastor's that have supported me by providing me guidance, Scripture, and prayer. They also provided me with references to trusted Christian mental health professionals! I believe that my mental health is just as important, if not more important, as my physical health. If I were physically sick or injured, I would seek professional guidance and treatment from a physician. My mental health is no different.

Since I have not made mention of medications, I want to clarify that I am in no way indicating that any of the programs and therapy I have received *replace* medication. Everyone and every situation is unique. Therefore, only a mental health professional can make that determination and develop a tailored treatment plan that is best for that individual. My family doctor and professional counselors have told me that sometimes using a combination of counseling and medication together is necessary, even if for a short time, to get the results someone may need to live a healthy and satisfying life. I don't want anyone to be fearful of seeking professional mental health treatment.

I believe that I would not be where I am today if it were not for my relationship with God, the counseling I have received, and the countless hours of personal inner work that I have done. I never want to return to the "old me." All the rage that I used to have inside was old trauma. Again, you can't just *think* your way out of the trauma. There has to be a healthy way to let it all out, or it will come out in a non-healthy manner.

Sometimes, I would ask my psychologist, Dr. Quirk, several questions that I wanted to know, because you know, he was the professional. I asked him if he could pinpoint the reason why people couldn't ultimately get along in a relationship, whether it be personal, family, stranger, or co-worker. He simply said, "Tammy, I think it comes down to personality disorders." I believe there is a lot of truth in what he said to me that day. Most people won't seek help, seek God, or try and change their life. My hope is that my story will encourage people to seek help if nothing more than for a better and healthier life! My goal is to help erase the stigma surrounding asking for help if you have had past traumas, a mental illness, lost your faith in God, or all of the above.

A few of my professional resources have told me that I had been suffering from Post-traumatic stress disorder (PTSD), and what I should do to overcome my symptoms. I learned that there had been a broadening of the definition of PTSD. Some people believe that PTSD is only associated with military personnel that battle with trauma due to their service, but PTSD can happen to anyone! The types of related trauma can include sexual assault, natural disasters, accidents, injuries, and life-threatening situations. I was not aware that you could have PTSD, even if the traumatic event didn't happen to you. Being a witness to a traumatic event can lead to PTSD symptoms. Just because you are involved in or witness these, doesn't mean that you will necessarily suffer from it. Lastly, PTSD symptoms may not occur immediately. To me, this is an excellent example of why I believe that seeking the assistance of mental health professionals is so important.

You are why I wrote this book. My heart was to connect with you through sharing my life experiences and to bring about mental health awareness. I pray that my story has encouraged you, draws you closer to our Lord and Savior, Jesus Christ, and has given you a new perspective and understanding of the importance of your mental health.

You may be wondering where I am today in my journey. Celebrate with me as I share how God has been faithful and blessed me beyond anything I could have imagined before I began my recovery, and I leave you with one final story.

As I mentioned previously, I didn't start dealing with past issues until I stopped working at a regular job. I consider myself extremely fortunate that Clint has provided me a life where I can *choose* to stay at home and not work. It has allowed me to focus on my recovery, self-care, and my marriage. Additionally, it has freed me to be able to things that I would have never dreamed to have been possible.

One of these things is that I can volunteer at a local hospital in the neonatal intensive care unit (NICU) as a "cuddler" to the preemies and newborns. It is especially meaningful since I was a preemie! Volunteering has been one of the most rewarding things that I have ever done. When I am helping take care of these babies, it makes me wonder if it was how my family felt going in to see me when I was a preemie. I can't quite put it into words the emotions I have when I am volunteering in the NICU. It is something that you would have to experience for yourself. The rewards far exceed the time I spend volunteering. While skin-on-skin contact may be beneficial for the health of the babies, there are times that I wonder whether I benefited more from my volunteer shift than the babies!

Within the last year, I had the opportunity to resume modeling after having not done it for several years. I modeled wedding gowns in a fashion show at my local civic center. When the agency contacted me for the show, I thought to myself, "Not bad for someone in their mid-forties!" I had fun during the show, but it had been a while since I had modeled on a runway, and my anxiety got in the way a little bit. I pushed myself through my anxiety, and I had a renewed confidence after completing the show. I'm not sure how many more modeling opportunities that I will have in the future, or if I will even continue, but I know that I've accomplished more than I ever thought I would when I began modeling.

Clint and I recently built a home in a beautiful, pedestrian-friendly neighborhood in Huntsville. I decided that I wanted to start my own part-time errand service business in our small community. When you don't have to work, I think it makes a big difference in your attitude and how you approach work. For example, in the past, I *had* to work to pay bills and make ends meet. Now, I work because it allows me to help others and to keep myself busy doing something positive. The best part is that I get to choose my hours and get paid to do it! I work part-time because I still need time to get my errands done and to be available to do things with Clint.

Clint and I met at the age of forty-one. We were married just a few months before he retired from serving on active duty in the Army for twenty-three years. Clint still works for the federal government, but now he serves as a Department of the Army civilian employee. Now that he is retired from active duty, he has a more predictable schedule, is home more often, and has more freedom in scheduling his time off. He has made a lot of sacrifices and had enormous responsibilities during his life. I am so proud of him for his dedication and service!

Some of the best advice I've ever heard is, "No one is going to be on their deathbed one day wishing they had spent another day at the office!" My point is no one is guaranteed tomorrow. We didn't meet each other until we were middle-aged. We made a vow to each other when we married that we were going to live life to the fullest possible, one that we had always dreamed of having one day and that we were not going to let anyone or anything to get in the way. I am not alluding to you that our lives are perfect, because we are both flawed, and life simply isn't perfect, no matter what. However, we made a commitment to God and ourselves to place our relationship with each other second, only to God.

Saying "no" to things and people is necessary for self-care and living life intentionally. It is especially true since Clint and I are both recovering codependents. We have had to apply what we learned in recovery and to be intentional in our decisions. Everything counts, and time doesn't wait on anyone. We try to make the most of our time, and not take it for granted. All we have is *now*. If we are too worried about yesterday, and too busy looking out into the future that may never come, we are missing the present, 100 percent of the time. The present is a gift, and that is why it's called the *present*!

One thing that comforts me in life is listening to music. I enjoy a wide variety of music genres, and my favorite artists within those genres can span decades! Throughout my life, I have listened to and enjoyed rock, pop, country, classical, alternative, metal, hip-hop, rap, R&B, easy-listening, jazz, and, of course, Christian. I have loved seeing Christian music over the years expand into nearly every one of the above genres. I listen to Christian music a majority of the time these days, and it is the most uplifting to me. My current favorite Christian songs are: "You Say" by Lauren Daigle, "From the

Inside Out" by for KING & COUNTRY, "Even If" by MercyMe, and "Reckless Love" by Cory Asbury.

Speaking of music, Clint and I enjoy dancing from time to time. As you know, I have loved to dance all of my life. A couple of years ago, I talked Clint into taking ballroom dance classes. Clint was hesitant, at first, as he had *never* danced in his life. Clint has some social anxiety, and since dancing usually involves being in "social" environments, it is something he had never wanted to do. Once we started taking lessons, he began enjoying it, especially since the lessons were either just the two of us or in a small group of people in the dance studio. It was a great way to spend quality time together, and it was something we could do for fun. Our dance instructor, Harold, was patient with us and made our classes so much fun. Even though we are not currently taking lessons, we stay in touch with Harold and consider him a good friend.

They broke the mold when they made Clint! Clint continually encourages and supports me. I am not an easy person to live with, at times, and I'm sure there are times that I make it hard to love me. I don't say that in a way to put myself down, but I say it in a way that I am humbled by it. I am sure that none of us are *always* lovable or easy to live with at times.

Clint and I do things to feed our relationship with God, each other, and our recovery. Clint and I both love to read, so we usually have at least a couple of books that we are each reading at any given time. We love to watch Pastor Craig Groeschel's sermons at Life.Church Online, and attend our local church, though we aren't there every time the doors are open. We regularly watch Dr. Phil and listen to his podcasts. It was through the *Dr. Phil Show* that we learned about Onsite. We watched episodes where Dr. Phil would refer guests to Onsite and have Miles Adcox, the owner, and CEO of Onsite, on his show. We are big fans of Dr. John M. Gottman. If you haven't heard of him, he is a famous psychological researcher and clinician. He has done extensive work for over four decades on marital stability. We also regularly attend Co-Dependents Anonymous (CoDA) meetings.

One of the things I told Clint before he married me was that he was going to "date me" for the rest of our lives. Courtship shouldn't end because you are married. He agreed, and he still dates me and *will* continue to do so! Clint does a lot of things with me, and we take time out for regular date nights. Yes, it is easier with no kids in the house. There isn't anything Clint wouldn't do for me. Many people have told me that I got lucky finding a man like Clint, but I believe that this is only partially true. If you thought this, then

I'm also here to step on your toes a little bit and tell you that if you don't have a spouse that is doing some of these things, it's because you didn't require him to do them in the beginning. I firmly believe this to be true. One of the first things I learned in recovery is that we teach people how to treat us! For example, I taught Clint what I needed to feel loved (being dated), and since he loves me, he does his best to do those things for me.

I remember the time that I thanked Clint's mother, Nedra, for raising a son that is a gentleman and that I now benefit significantly from their influence! Some serious effort, work, and love were invested by my husband's parents to make him the man he is today, and I feel they deserve a lot of credit for how they raised him! That love and effort comes out in the way that my husband treats me every day.

Clint and I are approaching our fifth anniversary, and we have been blessed with two granddaughters, Lydia, and Renesmee! These are by Clint's two sons, Ryan, who is married to Naomi, and Aaron, who is married to Hannah. We are thankful to have such wonderful daughters-in-law and mothers to our grandchildren. For our entire marriage, we have had a broken relationship with Clint's daughter, Rebekah, and have only seen her twice in nearly five years. For three years, we made numerous attempts to reconcile our relationship with her. Eventually, we had to release ourselves from the situation. We are thankful that our God is a God of love and restoration. We have been able to restore our relationship with Clint's youngest son, Aaron, and we are thankful for that relationship. Our relationship with Clint's mother, Nedra, is the best it has been since we were married. She is currently going through a difficult time, as Clint's father, Bill, has dementia.

I am here to tell you that through all of the knowledge I've learned and the recovery work I've completed, my life is still far from perfect. I still struggle daily. I still have bouts with anxiety. I still have feelings of self-doubt. I think this is only natural, but the difference is that I now possess the knowledge and have the right tools in my toolbox to address these things properly. I have never been happier in my life, and I am blessed beyond measure.

I have always tried to be health-conscious, but I place a greater emphasis on my diet, exercise, and sleep now that I understand how impactful it can be on my mental health! I'm confident that almost everyone understands the physical benefits of exercise, but what about the psychological benefits? Exercise is a valuable tool in your toolbox, especially for those of us that struggle with stress and anxiety. When we exercise or do other physical activities, our bodies produce endorphins, which can lead to decreased tension levels, increase our mood and self-esteem, and help improve our sleep. Learning these things, I've incorporated regular exercise as a part of my recovery.

For your safety, please see your family doctor before you begin any exercise program to ensure that you can safely exercise. Additionally, your doctor will be able to recommend what forms of exercise may be best for you, based upon your medical history. Now, I don't exactly qualify, nor would I ever call myself a "gym rat," but I do my best to exercise a few times per week. I know that someone out there is probably thinking, "Tammy, you're still young and healthy, you don't have kids or work a regular full-time job, so it's easy for you to tell me that I need to exercise." Again, please allow me permission to step on your toes a little bit by saying that there is usually a sidewalk nearby, and it's free! I say this because you don't need fancy workout clothes or a gym membership to obtain the benefits of exercise. I'll admit, I do have a gym membership, but I view it as an investment in myself, especially at less than $1/day. Even though I have a gym membership, the sidewalk is literally a hop, skip, and a jump away.

When the weather is cooperative, I usually prefer to go outside for a walk through our neighborhood over going to the gym. When it comes to finding the time, I ask that you take a quick inventory of how you spend your day. When I looked at my typical day, I found that I was easily spending more time on social media or watching my favorite show every day than I was exercising. Did I enjoy those things? Did I do those things to "unwind" or reduce stress? Absolutely, but when I was honest with myself, a quick walk was not only much more effective at helping me "unwind," but it provided me with all of the additional physical and mental benefits at the same time. Clint will occasionally join me for a walk in the evening or on the weekend. We both enjoy these opportunities to spend quality time together and talk about whatever is on our minds while enjoying a beautiful day.

I get it! Starting to exercise and work out is difficult. Not only finding the time, but our bodies have a way of letting us know just how long it has been since we last exercised. I find that my body tends to provide me very distinct clues of this, especially as I get older. Did I mention that I took a Zumba class recently at the gym after not having attended one for a couple of years? The good news is that I didn't die, but the bad news was that I was sore for a few days. Before I started back doing more intensive exercise, such as a Zumba class, I scheduled an appointment to see my doctor. In addition to giving me a thumbs up for doing more vigorous exercise, I was told that exercising is the single most important thing I can do for my anxiety. When it comes down to it, exercising *and* eating clean is the answer to a multitude of health issues!

I have done plenty of personal research on the topic of eating. By no means am I a nutritionist or health expert, but I can share with you what has worked for *me* when I have actually stuck to eating healthy! We are all prone to "fall off the wagon" from time to time! Again, I urge you to seek advice from your physician before making any changes to your diet. Certain health conditions require specific nutritional requirements.

One thing that I have noticed since I started eating healthier is that when I eat something unhealthy, it makes me feel sick because my body isn't accustomed to eating it! The healthier I eat, the more critical it is for me to stay away from unhealthy foods. I'm not one to try the latest diet regimen, partly because I believe in balance and sustainability. I will certainly lose weight if I eliminate certain things from my diet, but is it truly healthy for *me*? Is this something that can or should be eliminated from *my* diet? What happens if I incorporate it back in, even in moderation? These are the types of questions I ask myself before making any changes to my diet. One thing I have tried to incorporate is intermittent fasting. What this means is that I try to eat all of my meals in an 8-hour window and fast for the other sixteen-hours. I don't always do this daily, but I try to stick to this as much as I can. For *me*, I know that I feel much better on the days that I incorporate intermittent fasting.

I eat a lot of proteins, veggies, and healthy fats. I stated earlier that I am not the best cook, so I usually eat frozen vegetables that I can steam in the microwave. Did I mention that I don't like to do dishes, either? My first choice is to opt for green vegetables. I heard a saying that stuck with me years ago about eating green vegetables. It says, "So fresh and so green will make me so lean!" When it comes to healthy fats, I like to eat avocados, olive oil, and nuts. Diabetes and heart problems are common in my family. My risk of developing these health conditions can be significantly reduced or possibly eliminated by my food choices. I have read and been told by my doctor and therapists that certain foods and ingredients have been identified to contribute to a reduction in your sleep quality, mood, and even some mental health conditions, such as depression and anxiety. This information alone was enough for me to start paying closer attention to what I was eating!

Some of you may be thinking to yourself, "I don't know Tammy, I am just such a mess, I don't even know if God could use me!" If this is you, let me tell you something, if you don't get anything else out of this book or my story, understand that if God can use me, he can use anyone! I don't say this to sound cliché. I believe it! The Bible is filled with people who failed that God used to accomplish amazing things and to bring Him Glory, including Noah, Abraham, Isaac, Jacob, David, and even the disciples!

I will admit that when I messed up in my past, I tended to go off the deep end and jump off the top rope, as they say! What I am telling you is that if that describes you, then we can relate. We have a connection through our experiences. I believe that this connection is important. Who do you think can fully reach a person that is going through or recently been divorced? I am not saying that your *never* divorced pastor, counselor, or friend can't help, but I believe that someone who has had been through that same divorce experience can more easily make that connection. I am thankful that not everyone can relate directly to my story for obvious reasons! Let's all take a moment to thank God for what *did not* happen in our lives!

We are here for a reason, and we all have a purpose. My life could have been over when I came into the world as a preemie! My life could have been over if I had made the decision that I didn't want to live anymore. My life could have been over countless times in my life. But you know what, it is *not* over! It isn't over for me, and it isn't over for you. It's over when God says it's over! Always remember that God has a purpose and a plan for you*! "For I know the plans I have for you," declares the Lord, "plans to prosper you and not to harm you, plans to give you hope and a future." (Jeremiah 29:11 – NIV)*

I thank God for my life journey and the opportunity to tell *my* story. Hopefully, many chapters are remaining in my life! Lord, use me up until you can use me no more! I am an overcomer! *"And they overcame him by the blood of the Lamb and by the word of their testimony, and they did not love their lives to the death." (Revelation 12:11 – NKJV)* You can have that life, and it can start right now! You don't need anyone else's permission!

As I write these final words of my book, Clint and I are under a Stay at Home order as a result of the COVID-19 outbreak. We pray that everyone is safe and for those that are on the front lines battling this unseen threat to our Nation. I understand that this situation is affecting everyone in different ways, and we are all doing our best during this uncertain time. My recovery has greatly assisted me in personally handling this difficult situation. The tools I have learned have helped me to keep my anxiety in check and maintain my focus on the *now*. We are blessed that Clint has been able to telework from home. We are utilizing this *extra* time together to focus on our marriage and to complete the final editing of my story to you. I will leave you with this funny, but beautiful true story:

Our neighborhood is located directly adjacent to a large cemetery, Huntsville Memory Gardens, and is separated only by a small creek and tree line. The home we recently built is only a couple hundred yards from the cemetery, which also happens to be where Grandmama and Granddaddy are buried. Clint and I decided to purchase our burial plot in this cemetery, as well. One of the primary reasons for this is that we wanted to have everything "in order," and it would be one less thing for one of us or the kids to be concerned about when we pass. We chose to be cremated, with our remains placed inside a cremation monument. Because the cemetery is so close and our burial plot is near the tree line, Clint, and I jokingly tell people that we plan on being buried in our back yard!

Our cremation monument holds two urns and looks like a little house. From a distance with the black granite nameplate in the center, it strongly resembles a doghouse, although I prefer to call it our mini-condo. We decided not to pre-engrave our names and birthdates on the monument, as that seemed a little too "creepy" to us. What we like most about the location of our burial plot is that it is located along a winding pathway and at the end of "cul-de-sac"! I know I said this is a "funny" story, and it probably seems more dark than funny, but I had to give you the setup.

The reason I'm telling you this story is because a few months ago, my Uncle Jesse had a family member pass away. I attended the funeral, along with several of our other family members, in Huntsville Memory Gardens. Later, I found out that when my uncle was driving away from the cemetery, he pointed out our plots to my other family members in the car and said, "There's Tammy's doghouse over there!" I am not trying to downplay or make light of death. I am merely trying to pre-write the end of *my* story before I do pass one day, and how I want to be remembered. One of the things that I want to be remembered for is my humorous side, just like my Granddaddy. I want my family and friends that are left behind to re-tell this "doghouse" story at my memorial service. My cousin, Rebecca, said, "Oh, this story *will* be told!"

Friends, here's to writing your own story, and may it be just as colorful as mine! Make sure that you enjoy the ride and slide into heaven on two wheels!

Tammy Verge is available for book interviews and personal appearances. For more information contact:

Tammy Verge
C/O Advantage Books
P.O. Box 160847
Altamonte Springs, FL 32716
info@advbooks.com

To purchase additional copies of these books, visit our bookstore at:
www.advbookstore.com

Longwood, Florida, USA
"we bring dreams to life"™
www.advbookstore.com